THE MORAL PHILOSOPHY

OF SANTAYANA

THE

MORAL PHILOSOPHY

OF

SANTAYANA

Milton Karl Munitz

GREENWOOD PRESS, PUBLISHERS
WESTPORT, CONNECTICUT

The Library of Congress has catalogued this publication as follows:

Library of Congress Cataloging in Publication Data

Munitz, Milton Karl, 1913–
   The moral philosophy of Santayana.

   Reprint of the 1958 ed.
   Originally presented as the author's thesis,
Columbia, 1938.
   1. Santayana, George, 1863-1952--Ethics.
I. Title.
B945.S24M8 1972   191   72-7813
ISBN 0-8371-6530-X

Copyright 1958 by The Humanities Press, Inc.

Originally published in 1958
by The Humanities Press, New York

Reprinted with the permission
of The Humanities Press, Inc.

First Greenwood Reprinting 1972

Library of Congress Catalogue Card Number 72-7813

ISBN 0-8371-6530-X

Printed in the United States of America

FOREWORD

DR. MUNITZ's book needs no exposition, for with erudition and informed lucidity it explains itself. But the reader needs, perhaps, to be advised of the important way in which this study clarifies a subject in two senses important. Santayana is a major figure in contemporary culture; the interest attaches to this book that would attach to any considered study of any contemporary master. But Dr. Munitz's book happens to deal with an aspect of Santayana that is not only central to an understanding of that catholic and comprehensive thinker, but central also to any candid purview of the moral issues of our generation.

Dr. Munitz has wisely subordinated the many diverse facets of Santayana's thought, those varied provinces in which that philosopher has made distinguished contributions: his theory of knowledge, aesthetics, metaphysics, and literary criticism. He has taken for granted—as by this time one should take for granted—Santayana's felicity of phrase and constant poetry of utterance. He has accented the architectonic of his thought, his moral philosophy, though the careful reader will find in these closely written pages succinct, carefully documented references to all these matters.

But this book is not intended as an extended table of contents of Santayana's writings. It is a much more serious and a much more fruitful enterprise. A study of a philosopher, to be important, must itself be philosophical, and the virtue of Dr. Munitz's book lies in his presentation, at once devoted and detached, of the controlling intent and the dominant issues—moral issues—posed or implied by Santayana's thought. Does not the latter himself say "moral philosophy . . . is my chosen subject"?

Dr. Munitz examines his author on moral ground. He reveals in him the naturalist, the Aristotelian, studying the materials, in life and nature, for a life of reason expressed in science, religion, and social institutions. He reveals in him also the contemplative, who regards existence itself as an irrational accident and reason itself as precarious and conditioned; he shows him as the poet, skeptic, and spiritual anarchist who regards the achievement of spirituality as the freedom of turning the mind on the infinite realm of essence. Dr. Munitz finds grounds in Santayana for classifying him at once as a Buddhist saint and a Greek pagan, as a humanistic inquirer into the natural conditions of the good life and as a disillusioned quietist looking beyond good and evil to "a paradise where all things are crystallized into the images of themselves, and have lost their urgency and their venom."

To Santayana himself there does not seem to be any essential conflict between his Greek morality and his Buddhist-Christian detachment. But a philosopher does not always know himself best and it is a merit of an interpreter at once responsible and imaginative to elicit what is sometimes hidden from the philosopher himself, and from many unwary readers. Dr. Munitz discriminates and verifies in Santayana two divergent moralities: one worldly, naturalistic, humane, the other unworldly, ascetic, and Indian in character; one conceiving the will as chastened by experience and the world as the field for a possible rational happiness, the other differently chastened, differently disciplined, liberated to an ironic emancipation from the world and a contempt for it in favor of an "imaginative play with the non-existent," a free roaming among whatever essences may swim into the spirit's ken. From the point of view of this transcendental passing beyond good and evil, all finite existences are simply illustrations, beautiful or terrible, of pure being.

This duality in Santayana which Dr. Munitz so carefully documents and morally estimates, is a duality of all sensitive minds, who are torn between conceiving life as a moral opportunity and as a conversation, brief and brilliant, with eternal forms. Dr. Munitz, in assaying both strains in Santayana, touches upon a theme of tragic importance in our time and in any time. The hope and disillusions, the generous energy and the resigned, abnegating meditation of the human spirit, find their voice in Santayana. What this voice has said and how it has said it are made clearer in these responsible and sympathetic pages.

IRWIN EDMAN

New York City
April 12, 1939

ACKNOWLEDGMENTS

I WELCOME this opportunity to acknowledge my indebtedness for the assistance directly or indirectly received in the preparation of this essay. Professor Morris R. Cohen's inspired and brilliant lectures on "The Life of Reason," which I attended as an undergraduate, provided the original stimulus to my study of Santayana. The influence upon my general interpretation of Santayana, of the many suggestive insights and comments to which Professor F. J. E. Woodbridge has given expression, will be readily perceived in more than one instance in the following pages. I am especially indebted to Professor Irwin Edman, whose expert knowledge and sensitive, thorough understanding of Santayana's philosophy has been a constant source of illumination to me in my many conversations with him while this work was being written. His general unfailing kindness and encouragement have meant more to me than I can say. To Professor Ernest Nagel, of Columbia University, and to Professor Y. H. Krikorian, of the College of the City of New York, I am deeply grateful for friendly interest and sympathetic advice. Finally, to my friend Dr. Justus Buchler I am greatly obligated for careful reading of the manuscript and for many helpful suggestions and penetrating criticisms.

MILTON KARL MUNITZ

New York City
April 14, 1939

CONTENTS

KEY TO ABBREVIATIONS

BHMO	*Brief History of My Opinions* in "Contemporary American Philosophy," edited by G. P. Adams and W. P. Montague, Vol. II, New York, Macmillan and Co., 1930.
DL	*Dialogues in Limbo,* New York, Scribner's, 1925.
EGP	*Egotism in German Philosophy,* New York, Scribner's, 1916.
GTB	*The Genteel Tradition at Bay,* New York, Scribner's, 1931.
JPh	*Journal of Philosophy*
LP	*The Last Puritan,* New York, Scribner's, 1936.
LR	*The Life of Reason,* New York, Scribner's, 1905–6:
	Vol. I. *Introduction and Reason in Common Sense.*
	Vol. II. *Reason in Society.*
	Vol. III. *Reason in Religion.*
	Vol. IV. *Reason in Art.*
	Vol. V. *Reason in Science.*
LSP	"Lotze's System of Philosophy," Manuscript at Harvard University, 1889.
OS	*Obiter Scripta,* New York, Scribner's, 1936.
PR	*Interpretations of Poetry and Religion,* New York, Scribner's 1900.
PSL	*Platonism and the Spiritual Life,* New York, Scribner's, 1927.
RE	*The Realm of Essence,* New York, Scribner's, 1927.
RM	*The Realm of Matter,* New York, Scribner's, 1930.
RT	*The Realm of Truth,* New York, Scribner's, 1938.
SAF	*Scepticism and Animal Faith,* New York, Scribner's, 1923.
SB	*The Sense of Beauty,* New York, Scribner's, 1896.
SE	*Soliloquies in England,* New York, Scribner's, 1922.
STTMP	*Some Turns of Thought in Modern Philosophy,* New York, Scribner's, 1933.
TCWJ	*The Thought and Character of William James,* R. B. Perry. Boston, Little, Brown and Company, 1935.
TE	*The Works of George Santayana:* Triton edition, 14 vols. New York, Scribner's, 1936.
TPP	*Three Philosophical Poets,* Cambridge, Harvard University Press, 1910.
WD	*The Winds of Doctrine,* New York, Scribner's, 1913.

The abbreviations listed above, with the exception of JPh and TCWJ, refer to works by Santayana. For a complete bibliography of Santayana's published writings see the appendix to *Obiter Scripta.* For a bibliography of secondary material consult G. W. Howgate, *George Santayana,* University of Pennsylvania Press, 1939.

I

NATURALISM AND DUALISM

Central rôle of moral philosophy.—The chief problem of philosophy, according to Santayana, is an understanding of the "relation of man and of his spirit to the universe [SAF, p. viii]." His own writings, on the whole, are devoted to the essentially moral problem of understanding the conditions of life and estimating its possible goods. His contributions to ontology and the theory of knowledge are best viewed as outgrowths of an interest in exploring the environment in which the activities of life take place and of defining the status, limits, and uses of knowledge, so that the instruments and possible attainments of human life may thereby be made clear and intelligible. Thus the enterprise of carefully delineating the generic traits of reality is undertaken in order that an individual, endowed with a conscious moral life, may determine with respect to his habitat the nature and extent of his various allegiances. Santayana would follow the procedure of those first philosophers "who knew the world and cast a speculative glance at the heavens, the better to understand the conditions and limits of human happiness [LR,V, 217]." That the ultimate message of his own philosophy is a moral one is supported by his statements, for he writes:

moral philosophy . . . is my chosen subject [SE, p. 257]; it was happiness or deliverance, the supervening supreme expression of human will and imagination, that alone really concerned me. This alone was genuine philosophy [BHMO, pp. 248–49]; the hierarchy of goods, the architecture of values, is the subject that concerns man most. Wisdom is the first philosophy, both in time and authority; and to collect facts or to chop logic would be idle and would add no dignity to the mind, unless that mind possessed a clear humanity and could discern what facts and logic are good for and what not [LR, V, 217].

In saying that Santayana is primarily a moralist, it is necessary to indicate the sense in which that term should be understood and to distinguish it from one that it sometimes enjoys. It designates an interest in the conditions and ideals of human activity, rather than in preachment. Santayana sees the world as a stage and human life as a dramatic spectacle, the plot of which, if there is one, it is the part of wisdom to discover and, having discovered, to use in the intelligent direction of our lives for the realization of their ultimately genuine goods. The approach is markedly Greek in inspiration ("for moral philosophy we are driven back upon the ancients [LR,I, 31]") and different from the approaches of our own day, which are derived from Kantian, British empirical, and orthodox religious theories that put their respective emphases on rights and duties, approval and disapproval, and the observance of rules for righteous conduct. Its concern is, not with obligation, moral sense, or an apologetic for commandments authoritatively imposed and of supposedly supernatural origin, but rather with the attainment through free and conscious effort of intrinsically satisfying goods within a lifetime bounded by the natural limits of birth and death. Its historical affinities, in this respect at any rate, are with Socrates, Plato, and Aristotle, not with the Romans, Hebrews, or Germans (cf. LR, V, 227), for it seeks to define the conditions of happiness rather than of righteousness. The latter consists in an observance of rules of behavior that at its best conduces to harmonious living. Yet if righteousness itself is made the final good, instead of its being judged in terms of what goods it makes possible, then, Santayana maintains, we have a slavish subservience to means instead of to ends. And "fanaticism [which] consists in redoubling your effort when you have forgotten your aim [LR, I, 13]" is, as likely as not, the result of such an attitude.

It seldom occurs to modern moralists [he writes] that theirs is the science of all good and the art of its attainment; they think only of some set of categorical precepts or some theory of moral sentiments, abstracting altogether from the ideals reigning in society, in science, and in art. They deal with the secondary question What ought I to do? without having answered the primary question, What ought to be? . . . They divide man into compartments and the less they leave in the one labelled "morality" the more sublime they think their morality is; and sometimes pedantry and scholasticism are carried so far that nothing but an abstract sense of duty remains in the broad region which should contain all human goods [LR, I, 30; cf. WD, p. 139].

Furthermore, it is the ultimate demand that existence and human life justify themselves in terms of the values they might sustain that distinguishes the philosophy of Santayana from systems of positivism, which regard the mere description of facts as the sole form of possible intellectual inquiry; and from philosophies of romanticism, which see in mere "life" or action the sole excuse for living. Neither blind action without conscious foresight of desirable ends nor the nearsighted recording of whatever happens to exist can in itself, without further reflection upon its possible values, justify itself as against the persistent demand that we account for what we are doing in terms of the ends that may be served. Of course even action that is habitual or impulsive (unenlightened by conscious intent) and thought that is concerned with the unraveling of causal regularities in nature may yield moments of unanticipated pleasure or intellectual satisfaction and practical control. But to be aware of these is at once to perceive their justifying values. Instead of resting satisfied with an implicit and unexpressed justification of action, the examined life proceeds to make preferences and ideals explicit objects of critical analysis. Moral philosophy is simply the conscious and attentive consideration of human activity, practical and theoretic, that would deepen, insure, and estimate its relative values, relations, and consequences in experience.

Given the prior and originally inexplicable facts of existence and activity, human reason looks, not for the ultimate grounds of creation, but for the purposes or ends that the already existent or the naturally possible can serve. Happiness, the general name for all positive human values, as Aristotle long ago pointed out, itself needs neither justification nor praise. It is that in terms of which other things must be justified or estimated. This emphasis upon moral idealism has been one of the outstanding characteristics of Santayana's thought from the very beginning. As far back as 1889, in his doctoral thesis on *Lotze's System of Philosophy*, we find the following clear statement of this point:

Everybody will admit in one form or another that the primary facts of being whether they be axioms of thought, atoms of matter or the nature of God, are inexplicable and irreducible facts. The only sort of explanation we can find for them is their value, now they are here. We cannot say; this is the cause that brought the axioms, the atoms, or God into existence; we cannot see a reason why they were necessarily thus and not otherwise. All we can do is to discover a value in their actual constitution and result, and say, They are very good. This moral justification, this value of what we find to exist, is the only source of rationality in things. The mere regularity of events, the mere fact that things instead of happening only once happen again and again in the same ways does not explain the world or make it rational. Only the fact that these repetitions, these laws and given conditions, serve to bring about a worthy and happy consummation, that they enable us to live, to enjoy, and to produce and discover things of value in our eyes,—this alone is an explanation and justification of being [LSP, pp. 249 f.].

Moral philosophy, then, is for Santayana, as was dialectic for Plato, the supreme science. The delineation of values and the architecture of the specific structure of the good life constitute the ultimate interest of his thought.

Historical affinities and development of Santayana's philosophy.—In developing a philosophy that would indicate the general setting, instruments, and structure of the good life, Santayana looks, for his principles, to what he takes to be certain traditional orthodoxies in the history of thought. In a recent Preface to the Triton edition of his collected works he states that he would give expression in his ultimate philosophy to at least three of these traditional systems, since each is "humanly right in its own sphere, but wrong in ignoring or denying the equal human rightness of the other two [TE, I, ix]." These are: first, orthodoxy in natural philosophy, represented by the Greek naturalists before Socrates, by Spinoza, and by the whole of modern science; second, orthodoxy in morals, represented by Plato and by Aristotle, the first to formulate the conception of the life of reason; and third, orthodoxy in transcendental reflection, or the ethics of the contemplative spirit, represented by the schools of the Indians.

Santayana conceives the function of science to be an investigation of the structure of nature, scene of the genesis and the activity of all extended, living, and thinking beings. Nature is the object of animal exploration, the environing context for all practical and productive activity. To discover its actual constitution is the essential prerequisite for any serious theory of the good life. Plato and Aristotle formulated the classic principles that define rational morality, an ideal the foundation of which is the animal core of human nature, and the structure of which is a harmony achieved through the use of critical intelligence. Finally, the Indians, although they neglected to consider the principles of rational morality and scientific naturalism, were, in spite of this fact, experts in developing the philosophy of a contemplative spirit, of the means of attaining ultimate peace through resignation and insight (cf. SE, pp. 209–16).

Although Santayana here singles out the Greeks, Spinoza,

and the Indians for special emphasis, the reader of his writings will find that these do not represent the only sources that have influenced his thought. One may mention in addition, as equally prominent, certain aspects of Christian thought, British empiricism, and that form of mystical, otherworldly Platonism which, appearing in some dialogues of Plato and in the writings of Plotinus and Schopenhauer, is commonly recognized as being characteristically different from the Aristotelian tradition in the history of philosophy.

Confronted with these various sources of influence, questions concerning the consistency of the incorporated parts, their exact boundaries, and the extent of their mutual support naturally arise. Further complications enter into a consideration of the development of Santayana's thought, the shifting emphases that mark its various phases, and the special senses in which certain of its basic categories are often redefined and made to serve in new or altered contexts, in accordance with a shift in attention or allegiance to these various sets of principles. If we consider, for example, the entire body of Santayana's writings from the viewpoint of its moral interest, we shall find that these traditions or the philosophies for which they stand do not play an equally prominent rôle, nor are they invoked in the same way at all times. Important changes of mood and attitude, reflecting varying degrees of reliance upon or inspiration by these several traditions, mark the development of the philosophy in its expression over a period of some forty-three years, from the publication of the first volume of verse in 1894 to the latest writings culminating in *The Realms of Being*.

These changes may be viewed, in somewhat Hegelian manner, as falling into three different periods.[1] The first and earliest period, represented by writings such as *Lucifer* and

---

[1] This classification is based on a suggestion made by Santayana himself, as contained in a letter written to the author.

Sonnets and Other Verses, constituted the expression in verse of a spiritual philosophy at once pessimistic in its coloring and otherworldly in its sympathies (cf. BHMO, pp. 242–43; 246). Here was the first tentative appearance of an attitude to be recognized as post-rational in the *Life of Reason* (of the middle period), and therefore one to be smilingly overcome by the energetic hopefulness of the proponent of a rational ethics. Yet it was an attitude to which Santayana in later writings was in certain respects to revert, although this time with important modifications and refinements.

In the second or middle period, however, at a time when Plato and Aristotle were the dominant influences upon his thought, *The Life of Reason* portrayed the structure and content of moral ideals possible to enlightened individual and cultural behavior. In that work Santayana adopts the rôle of the critical moralist engaged in the task of clarifying and estimating the relative value of various characteristic ideals in art, science, government, and religion. His own interests in this work fall within the context of the morality of the rational life, inasmuch as an exercise in moral science itself forms part of a developed life of reason.

Finally in the third period, beginning about 1913, when he left this country to live in Europe, a period represented by such works as *Dialogues in Limbo, Platonism and the Spiritual Life,* and *The Realms of Being,* Santayana once more turns to a philosophy of the free spirit, this time attempting a synthesis of the two previous attitudes—pessimism (thesis) and humanism (antithesis). The ethics of the spiritual life is supported by a humanistic and naturalistic foundation, and at the same time exhibits a wider range of vision than in his earlier version. In contrast with a youthful pessimism that stoically defies the agonies inflicted by a cruel world and in contrast with an energetic hopefulness or "normal madness" of maturity that eagerly sets about to find happiness in the clarification and actualization of its ideals, the spirituality described in the later writings expresses at once the disillusionment and the peace that comes with a certain type of detachment. Protests are tempered by the realization that the spirit must be incarnate. Yet salvation is not to come primarily through the idealism of a narrowly conceived individual and social welfare (although certain basic principles of the life of reason are required in support of the free spiritual life), but rather through a resigned disintoxication, wherever possible, from the urgencies of practice, and a contemplative devotion to the immediacies revealed by liberated intuition. From the demands of will, which seeks its satisfaction in time and in the appropriation of matter (a necessary condition for life itself), we turn to what is the supreme attainment of the human spirit—the joy to be found in viewing natural existence under the form of eternity.

Naturalism and dualism.—Now, whether we consider Santayana's philosophy from the point of view of its development or from the point of view of its systematic principles, two of its strains or aspects will be found to emerge for special notice as constituting the source, respectively, of its strength and of its weakness. I refer to its comprehensive naturalism, reflecting a desire to present a circumspect combination of the ultimate truth and value of certain traditional naturalistic persuasions in thought and conduct, and its eclecticism, which in the end militates against that comprehensive and consistent naturalism by including certain doctrines which render the latter uncertain and equivocal. From one point of view, the moderation, inclusiveness, and sanity of Santayana's philosophy illustrate an undeniable accomplishment of his thought. He has been able, as perhaps few other contemporary philosophers have been, to present a successful restatement of certain orthodox positions that together combine to fill out a thoroughgoing naturalistic theory in metaphysics, methodology, and ethics.

One finds in his writings a theory of nature that provides an adequate and intelligible context for his theory of rational animality, for the phases of human progress in the characteristic institutions of civilization, and for the contemplative or spiritual life. One may use, if one wishes, the term "Aristotelian" to describe the general spirit and substance of this aspect of his philosophy. In it we find a just regard for the comprehensive unity and the variegated plurality that constitute the total background for all inquiry and action. This, then, is one side of Santayana's philosophy: naturalism in metaphysics, a realistic theory of scientific methodology that finds nature accessible to exploration and genuine discovery of efficacious structure, and a theory of the good life that pays equal attention to both the theoretic and the practical functions of intelligence. However, one also finds (and this I take to be the result of an eclecticism that goes beyond the bounds of consistency), the inclusion of certain doctrines which are antithetical to the naturalism as a whole. These doctrines include: an ontologic dualism which sets up a realm of essence as altogether independent of nature, a Platonic heaven of timeless universals having no intelligible connection with the realm of matter and from which it is divorced; an epistemological dualism which bears striking similarity to the characteristic epistemology of British empiricism, especially that of Locke, Hume, and Spencer, for which the only alternative to an ultimate skepticism is an animal faith that in reality does not render natural processes amenable to genuine investigation, but one which relies instead upon an opaque screen of essences to function as symbols for an underlying and unknowable realm of matter; and, finally, certain characterizations of the spiritual life which, instead of making it an eligible vocation within the life of reason, seem to ally it with what Santayana himself has called "post-rational systems of morality," thereby making it an escape from and despair of life rather than its fulfillment and consummation.

The historical affinities of the one aspect of Santayana's philosophy are to be found in Aristotle and Spinoza. Both avoid epistemological inquiries and the use of a transcendental method as an introduction to their systems; both develop a consistent and inclusive theory of nature; and both emphasize the liberating and practical values of reason. The historical affinities of the other aspect of Santayana's philosophy are to be found in the spirit of Platonism, Lockianism, and a curious mixture of Epicureanism and Catholicism. The first accounts for a sharp separation between nature and a transcendent realm of essences, the realm of evanescent material objects, and the realm of universal, eternal Ideas; the second for a sharp separation between the mind, its ideas, and an external world of material substances which those ideas can never reach, a distinction between appearances that are illusory and a realm of objects possessing real, internal essences; and finally, the third accounts for the post-rational aspects of the spiritual life, making of it an attempt, in effect, to escape from pressing moral problems and the supposedly illusory idealism of the worldly life by devotion to an otherworldly contemplation of essences. Let us consider briefly the respective procedures and metaphysical settings provided by these differing strains in Santayana's philosophy before turning to his moral philosophy of the life of reason and the spiritual life.

Realistic methodology.—A naturalistic theory starts with a common-sense recognition of the intimate, daily objects and events disclosed by ordinary human experience. An empirically denotative method, dealing throughout with these obvious facts of daily life and involving the correlative belief that such facts together with our modes of acquaintance with them are illustrations of natural events within a total natural framework, are basic to this aspect of Santayana's philosophy. Whatever theoretical illumination and clarification his philosophy contains, is postulated upon this initial subject matter. Santayana repeatedly insists upon this grounding in common sense as essential to his method. He says:

I have a great respect for orthodoxy; not for those orthodoxies which prevail in particular schools or nations, and which vary from age to age, but for a certain shrewd orthodoxy which the sentiment and practice of laymen maintain everywhere. I think that common sense, in a rough dogged way, is technically sounder than the special schools of philosophy, each of which squints and overlooks half the facts and half the difficulties in its eagerness to find in some detail the key to the whole. . . . My philosophy is justified, and has been justified in all ages and countries, by the facts before every man's eyes [SAF, pp. v, x].

These facts before every man's eyes are obvious, familiar, and unquestionable. Their existence and accessibility to investigation do not have to be guaranteed by any prior epistemological inquiry. For this subject matter consists of "the stars, the seasons, the swarm of animals, the spectacle of birth and death, of cities and wars [*ibid.*, p. x]," of the complex total of activities, institutions, beliefs, and ideals constituting human life in its multiform expressions and manifestations. These facts define the setting for practice and understanding.

In agriculture, chemistry, the mechanical arts, medicine, and war there is an implicit acknowledgment of a system of forces that must be dealt with either by way of submission or transformation, if life itself is to continue. And in this situation there is no "problem of knowledge" in the sense of explaining how knowledge is possible or of guaranteeing a belief in the existence of an external world through animal

faith or any other such means. The only legitimate problem
of knowledge with which science and philosophy are profit-
ably concerned is the practical and gradually solvable one of
refining and extending the knowledge we already possess of
the structure of natural processes. For "there is a knowledge
which common life brings even to savages and which study,
exploration and the arts can clarify and make more precise
[OS, p. 95]." Instead of beginning with a skeptical dissolution of knowledge into a bare intuition of essences, from
which the only return to the natural world is by means of a
blind animal faith, the procedure that actually adds to our
knowledge rather than casts doubt upon its possibility is one
that starts with already-given interpretations of identified objects in experience and then proceeds to clarify, systematize,
and render them more exact than they were.

Every deeper investigation presupposes ordinary perception and
uses some at least of its data. Every possible discovery *extends*
human knowledge. None can base human knowledge anew on a
deeper foundation or prefix an ante-experimental episode to experience [LR, V, 36].

In *Reason in Common Sense* and *Reason in Science* Santayana deals with those phases of the natural history of intelligence and those principles of scientific methodology
which contribute to or actually operate in the furtherance of
knowledge thus conceived. It is true that even in these
volumes there is intertwined with this analysis the elements
of a dualistic epistemology and ontology; we shall return to
this aspect later.

In *Reason in Common Sense* we have a consideration of
mental life with respect to the emergence of characteristic
psychological faculties in the race (or as recapitulated in the
individual), and the respective functions which such faculties
display in their interaction with one another and with the
natural environment antedating or surrounding them, which

they gradually learn to disclose or to modify. The genesis of reason is found in animal living, which Santayana denotes by the general term "feeling," represented on the cognitive side by sensation and imagination and on the motive side by impulse.

Just as impulse with regard to conduct lives in the immediate present of desire and its fulfillment, so too its cognitive analogue, imagination, is filled with its poetic visions, having no regard to their antecedents nor issues, nor indeed to its own fortunes as the expression of a living body. Its whole concern is with the represented world of its dreams. A step in the direction of reason occurs with the union of impulse and imagination. In itself each has what the other lacks: impulse has force, but is blind; imagination has vision, but is impotent. A rationally practical life begins when, by joining impulse and imagination, enlightenment is given to the former and practical efficacy to the latter.

Likewise, a rationally cognitive life develops when imagination begins to function in perception, memory, and a discovery of the causal mechanisms of nature. Perception identifies permanent objects, "concretions in existence," by noting the regular collocation of certain qualities in a single object or event. Memory, too, comes to give continuity, retentiveness, and wider scope to our experience; it serves as a practical refinement and means of employment of the images present in the mind, inasmuch as these now refer to past events. The final step in the cognitive discovery of the structure of natural objects takes place when the flux is rendered intelligible by a disclosure of its actual constitution. The world is then seen to be not only qualitatively rich and historically continuous, but also mechanically intelligible. The materials of a chaotic experience are classified, organized, and shorn of imaginative extensions and irrelevancies. Reflection and experience begin to make order of the original impressions of the mind when what belongs to a scientific view is recognized as such and not confused with those qualities with which a moralizing and mythologizing spirit has overlaid them.

The procedure of science which Santayana describes in *Reason in Science* is but the refined continuance of this cognitive discovery of the intelligible structure of the world and of man's place in it. For science is "nothing but developed perception, interpreted intent, common-sense rounded out and minutely articulated [LR, V, 307]." The more literal analysis that science provides is due to the fact that it follows the lead of its subject matter, verifies its hypotheses, and thus expresses the character and relations of objects in their own terms. Science is thus largely a matter of getting things properly said; it is ruled by language and dialectic, and its ideal goal is the expression, by means of these, of the truth about existence. Moreover, the knowledge yielded by science is grounded like every other mode of response in human nature and is relative to its conditions.

Yet this relativity of science to the instruments and faculties possessed by man for the investigation of nature does not affect the ultimate truth of the conclusions arrived at by those means (cf. LR, V, 315). All criticism of science is either valid, and hence contributes to the growth of science itself, or else is worthless. The only legitimate problem of knowledge is the extension of the knowledge we already have by the methods we already possess. For science is simply "common knowledge extended and refined. Its validity is of the same order as that of ordinary perception, memory, and understanding [LR, V, 37]." It is not possible to subvert the basis of science as an expression in human life of the intelligible constitution of nature and remain standing on any firmer ground. A transcendental criticism of knowledge as contrasted with a scientific extension of knowledge is "merely disintegrating and incapable of establishing a single positive truth [LR, V, 312]." For transcendentalism makes "the assumption (a wholly gratuitous one) that a spontaneous constructive intellect cannot be a trustworthy instrument, that appearances cannot be the properties of reality, and that things cannot be what science finds that they are [LR, V, 310]."

All this I take to be a recognition on Santayana's part of what in fact is the situation and the procedure wherein knowledge of any subject matter, any portion of natural existence, is acquired, extended, and communicated. It is this procedure which Santayana himself employs with such notable success in, for example, *The Life of Reason,* where his subject matter is the complex total of human institutions in their growth and ideal development. It is by directly examining the characteristic activities of man in society, religion, art, and science, that he is able to lay bare the historical, social, and psychological conditions of these activities and to suggest what might be the most effective content of their respective ideals. It is the same procedure that lends whatever intelligibility and verifiable truth there are to the analyses, made in the later writings, of the generic traits of natural existence.

Naturalistic metaphysics.—Complementary to Santayana's realistic procedure, which is grounded in common sense and which appeals to scientific methodology for its principles, is his naturalistic metaphysics. This metaphysics provides the ultimate setting for a methodology that is capable of a gradual discovery of nature's actual structure, and for a theory of human life in which the need for intelligent adjustment and the value of intellectual contemplation receive justifiable attention.

In using the term "naturalistic metaphysics," I am conscious of the fact that it is one which Santayana himself decidedly disowns. As he understands the term "metaphysics," it is "dialectical physics, or an attempt to determine matters of fact by means of logical or moral or rhetorical constructions [SAF, p. vii; cf. RM, pp. 5–6]." In that sense, of course, he is justified in rejecting the term as a description of that candid and unprejudiced analysis of the fundamental traits of existence which he would provide. And I think that he is justified in rejecting that description, in so far as the theory he presents is genuinely naturalistic; although, to the extent that it also contains elements of a radical ontologic dualism, it would seem that metaphysics in precisely the sense he would disown is characteristic of it. At any rate, for the time being I am using the term not in Santayana's sense but in the same sense in which Professor Lamprecht employs it in his excellent article "Naturalism and Agnosticism in Santayana" (JPh, XXX [1933], 562), as a name for

the kind of reflection which is to be found in the unnamed work of Aristotle to which the term happened to be applied. In that sense metaphysics is a body of "first principles" about existence which we find to be warranted by observation and experiment . . . a systematic statement of the fundamental assumptions that lie at the base of any and all sciences about existence, provided that we have made those assumptions explicit and have tested them out by all the tests by which any principles can be tested.

I am using the term "naturalistic metaphysics" in the same sense in which I think that the systems of Aristotle, Spinoza, and Dewey may properly be designated as examples of it (even though Santayana in his special analysis of Dewey's system, for example, seems to think such a term a contradictory one). What I take to be Santayana's own naturalistic metaphysics will be implicitly defined by the following brief exposition, based on an admittedly selective interpretation of his various writings. I shall reserve for later discussion those points (also to be found in the works of Santayana) which seem to proceed from another context and which weaken or annul this fundamental naturalism.

Just as a beginning with common sense involves an avoidance of transcendental epistemology and, as a concomitant of that avoidance, an attempt to get back to the natural world after we have found ourselves left only with ideas, essences, or concretions in discourse, so a beginning in metaphysics involves an avoidance of the problem of creation. This means that we start with nature rather than with a Realm of Essence, for if we start with the latter we need a theory of creation to bridge the gap between that realm and the realm of matter. In beginning with nature we make no attempt to go behind it in order to account for its existence, nor even leave the way open for such a question; we simply investigate its evident and characteristic traits as they are found in our experience. That existence is irrational in the sense that we can never find any ultimate grounds or reasons for it, grounds or reasons that might lie beyond or behind nature, is a point that Santayana constantly insists upon. Reasons, grounds, creation, and ideals are to be found assuredly *within* nature; yet they cannot themselves be predicated of nor assumed with respect to anything that might exist outside of nature, as bearing upon it. For whatever relation such an existence might have to nature, be it logical, physical, or moral, would make of it but an extension of or an element within a more inclusive totality that would contain them both. And "nature" is simply the name for this most inclusive, ultimate totality.

Santayana's position on this subject affords a close similarity to Spinoza's proofs for the unity of Substance. Santayana's ontology of the Realms of Being in his later writings, however, is in many respects a departure from this conception, since those realms, instead of being viewed as attributes of a unified substance, take on the status of separate and independent domains. In naturalistic metaphysics, then, nature forms a single system, a unified whole. To speak of "the world" is "to set the problem for all natural philosophy, and in a certain measure to anticipate the solution of that problem; for it is to ask how things hang together, and to assume that they do hang together in one way or another [TPP, p. 22; cf. SE, p. 213; RM, pp. 24–25]."

The unity of nature is no more impressive, however, than is the combination presented by nature of mutation and recurrence, of change and constancy, of the flux of particulars and the endurance of a stable structure. When Democritus combined the insight of both Heraclitus and Parmenides and tried to account for the elements of both change and permanence by his materialism and mechanism, he hit upon a notion that has been the inspiration of naturalistic systems ever since. Santayana's admiration for the spirit and ideal of Democritean physics is made evident in his earlier work, *The Life of Reason,* as well as in *Dialogues in Limbo.*

The way Santayana incorporates that notion in his theory of nature, however, is not always uniform. Sometimes it becomes synonymous with an emphasis on the fact that in order to understand any natural subject matter one must discover "constant parts" and "constant laws." The ideal of mechanism becomes simply another name for intelligibility.

Mechanism is not one principle of explanation among others. In natural philosophy, where to explain means to discover origins, transmutations, and laws, mechanism is explanation itself [LR, I, 17].

At other times his notion of mechanism is reminiscent of that form of metaphysics which, in putting its emphasis on matter in motion, seems to relegate the facts of life, mind, and value to the sphere of appearances, thus recalling the "billiard-ball physics" of the nineteenth century and the mechanistic naturalism then so prevalent. As we shall see, this latter interpretation (to be found especially in certain passages of *The Life of Reason*) is in reality a departure from a genuinely inclusive and consistent naturalism, setting up, as it does, a dualism between the mechanical features of the world and the "symbolic dreams" of man's conscious, moral life.

In Santayana's later writings, of which *The Realm of Matter* is the crucial example, the notion of mechanism, even in the first of the above senses, receives less attention and yields in emphasis to materialism. In these writings "matter" or "substance" serves as the general name for that which is responsible for all action, productivity, creation, and efficacy in nature. And Santayana's emphasis upon this notion of substance is fundamental to his theory of nature, for it asserts "the dominance of matter in every existing being, even when that being is spiritual [RM, p. 100]." What the assertion of such dominance implies is clearly expressed by Santayana in his essay on "Dewey's Naturalistic Metaphysics." For, he tells us there, on the material framework that the notion of substance provides

it is easy to hang all the immaterial objects, such as words, feelings, and ideas, which may be eventually distinguished in human experience. We are not compelled in naturalism, or even in materialism, to ignore immaterial things; the point is that any immaterial things which are recognized shall be regarded as names, aspects, functions, or concomitant products of those physical things among which action goes on. . . . Naturalism may, accordingly find room for every sort of psychology, poetry, logic, and theology, if only they are content with their natural places [OS, pp. 214–15].

To a consistent and vigorous materialism all personal and national dramas, with the beauties of all the arts, are no less natural and interesting than are flowers or animal bodies. . . . The materialistic way of thinking . . . may be extended to the most complex and emotional spheres of existence [TPP, pp. 67–68].

Taking the fact of productivity as central, a concept involved in beginning with the notion of substance or matter, one may then render intelligible the way in which essence, life, spirit, and truth are involved in the dynamic flux of existence, and may see these elements in their proper context. For "one and the same flux of events exemplifies now one and now another of these realms of being or variously impinges upon them [RM, p. vi]." The realm of essence then becomes simply the realm of imagined objects, the totality of all possible themes of thought, discourse, logic, and fancy. Instead of considering essences, as Santayana generally does, to be ontologically antecedent objects that subsist prior to existence, in a naturalistic view they are regarded as natural creations or poetic themes in the etymological sense of the word, for they are products of the imagination, structures embodied in the limitless languages that the mind can construct, forms that a fertile imagination can freely contrive. To see essences in this way is to see the "eternal" in its true setting of the temporal and the existent. Such a naturalistic view of essence we find Santayana suggesting with greater definiteness in his earlier writings, especially in the chapter on "Dialectic" in *Reason in Science,* than in his later works. This view, for instance, receives only occasional mention in *The Realm of Essence,* where the dominant emphasis rests upon the ontologic status of essence as a separate realm, entirely independent of and severed from the realm of matter.

If essences, as revealed by logic, grammar, sensation, and poetic fancy, have material roots and sources in nature, the same is not less true regarding those portions of nature which we call life, spirit, and truth. A naturalistic view of these opposes the "noble ambiguities of idealism," which denies the priority of substance to life, consciousness, and reflection. For naturalism is but the extension of the common-sense objection against all subjectivism in "regarding nature as the condition of mind and not mind as the condition of nature [LR, I, p. 104; cf. EGP, pp. 167–68]." Nature is the source of life and mind as well as of stones and plants. The former illustrate her productivity no less than the latter.

To say that matter, as it truly exists, is inert or incapable of spontaneous motion, organization, life, or thought, would be flatly to
contradict the facts: because the real matter, posited in action, and
active in our bodies and in all other instruments of action, evidently
possesses and involves all those vital properties. . . . Even the
thinnest creations of spirit, therefore, are products of the realm of
matter, and possible only within it [RM, p. 137, 84].

What we call life, mind, and spirit, are simply the forms,
or in Santayana's language, the tropes that substance assumes
when it reaches certain degrees of complexity. The differences
between what Santayana calls the psyche and the spirit are
differences in the level of organization and function that we
find in living beings. The psyche, or psychical life, is the
"specific form of physical life, present and potential, assert-
ing itself in any plant or animal [RM, p. 139]." It denotes
the level of activity attained in those products of nature that
are engaged in nutrition, reproduction, and the satisfaction
of animal impulses. Spirit, on the other hand, denotes the
level of activity attained in thought and feeling, the type of
behavior we designate as conscious.

Everything truly conscious or mental—feeling, intuition, intent—
belongs to the realm of spirit. We may say of spirit, but not of the
psyche, that its essence is to think [RM, p. 139].

Whether we consider psychical life or mental life, the psyche
or the spirit, those terms denote types of function, rather
than immaterial substances over and above material conditions and supposedly endowed with material powers. To construe them in the latter way is pure mythology. Neither life
nor mind are disembodied powers that in some mysterious
manner influence and direct their bodily instruments. They
are rather powers, latent or realized, in bodies themselves.
The terms matter and substance, in their Aristotelian meanings, may be used in this connection to describe the relation
between the psyche and the spirit. For the psyche, itself a
union of matter and form and thus a substance in the sense

of their conjunction, is with respect to the spirit its material condition. Yet with respect to the body, which in turn is its material condition, the psyche constitutes a form of activity that is realized when its material conditions reach a characteristic degree of complexity (cf. SE, p. 221).

From this point of view there is no "problem" of the relation of inorganic matter to animate or conscious life, of the body to the mind. We do not start with two substances and seek for their reconciliation or joint operation. "If we isolate the terms mind and body and study the inward implication of each apart, we shall never discover the other [LR, I, 206]." To escape the sophistications in which some forms of metaphysics become involved—those starting with the discriminated elements of natural substances or events and seeking somehow to solve the problem of creation by accounting for their reunion into those same substances—it is better to begin with the recognition of the naturally created fact, its obvious properties and characteristic relations. Like Spinoza's beginning with the unquestioned axiom that man thinks, Santayana insists we are "constrained merely to register as a brute fact the emergence of consciousness in animal bodies [BHMO, p. 253]." We then recognize that

consciousness . . . is the expression of bodily life and the seat of all its values. . . . Thought is . . . a link in the chain of natural events; for it has determinate antecedents in the brain and senses and determinate consequents in actions and words [LR, I, 207–8].

What becomes important, then, are the implications which the recognition of this evident fact of animate and conscious life possesses for a theory of nature. The truth about nature cannot disregard the fact that nature as easily gives birth to organisms that think and feel as to stars that move. Nor can the laws that describe the behavior of the latter exhaustively describe those of the former. The human body possesses certain physical properties which permit it to be classed, for certain analytical purposes, in the same class with stars and stones. But its obvious differences from the latter prevent the reduction of all its properties to a like treatment.

Movement could never be deduced dialectically or graphically from thought nor thought from movement. Indeed no natural relation is in a different case. Neither gravity, nor chemical reaction, nor life and reproduction, nor time, space, and motion themselves are logically deducible, nor intelligible in terms of their limits. The phenomena have to be accepted at their face value and allowed to retain a certain empirical complexity [LR, I, 208].

What Santayana intends by the use of the category "truth" in its relation to natural existence is best understood as consisting of the ideal standard of scientific investigation, the complete and accurate description of the structure of natural processes. As such an ideal it has an intelligible status in guiding inquiry to an eventual disclosure of the laws of nature. It defines the ideal quality which would be possessed by those statements reporting what is, what has been, or what will be with regard to anything whatsoever in existence. In this sense the truth "properly means the sum of all true propositions, what omniscience would assert [RT, p. vi]." Truth is an eventual property of propositions verified in the procedures of common sense or science. "For truth, at the intelligible level where it arises, means not sensible fact, but valid ideation, verified hypothesis, and inevitable, stable inference [LR, I, 201]." This, then, is one natural context in which truth (or its opposite, error) may be discussed—the context of inquiry and within it the claims of various assertions to report what is the case.

Santayana, however, also uses the term in a somewhat different sense, to denote "the whole ideal system of qualities and relations which the world has exemplified or will exemplify [RT, p. vi]"; the actual structure and forms which natural existence embodies in events and substances, whether those forms are disclosed to human cognition or not. In this sense the truth is not a matter primarily of verifiable discourse, the ideal of cognitive inquiry, but an ontological trait of natural subject matter, the fact of its possessing determinate structures (cf. RT, p. 39). Truth is a dimension of existence, in so far as existence takes on form and exhibits some specific order. As such, the truth, in the sense of the structure of the world, is concomitant and coextensive with nature's material powers, causal efficacy, and productive energies. That nature is productive and that nature in virtue of this productivity also brings into existence objects of determinate constitutions and qualities, and that each of these facts is in its own way an irreducible and ultimate trait of natural existence, is what Santayana seems to me to be insisting upon when he describes the matter and truth of existence. Like Spinoza's attributes of extension and thought, his use of theological language in ascribing Omnificence and Omniscience to God (cf. OS, pp. 280–97) recalls the same basic points in naturalistic metaphysics.

For such metaphysics, to summarize, nature is the matrix of whatever has being in any way. "The word nature has many senses; but if we preserve the one which etymology justifies, and which is the most philosophical as well, nature should mean the principle of birth or genesis, the universal mother, the great cause, or system of causes, that brings phenomena to light [TPP, pp. 56–57]." Nature is the set of conditions for animate and inanimate objects, for seasons and stars, for good and bad. It is the great cosmic theater wherein all forms and kinds of being play their individual yet related rôles. Nature is dynamic, a matter of beginnings and endings, of potentialities and actualities, of growth and decay. Nature is as much the seat of values and ideals (since man who is a part of nature may experience values and strive for ideals) as of mechanism and blind causation. It is as thoroughly qualitative as it is quantitative, as much as logical as it is physical. The sphere of nature is the unified totality of whatever it produces and contains. All distinctions found within this universe are discoveries of its diversely qualified and related contents. It is a universe whose traits are genuinely discoverable by piecemeal analysis and whose categories are the basic predicates of its individual substances and growth processes.

Transcendentalism and agnosticism.—In some portions of *Reason in Common Sense* and *Reason in Science* and more especially in the later work, *Scepticism and Animal Faith,* Santayana develops a theory of knowledge which by its procedure and conclusions serves to render equivocal the naturalism of his philosophy. The procedure is that of transcendentalism, the conclusion—agnosticism. Santayana in these discussions takes over the problems bequeathed to modern philosophy by Locke, Berkeley, and Hume, and seeks an answer to those problems in terms of the assumptions common to the characteristic epistemologic inquiries of these philosophers. The result is no more satisfactory than the conclusions arrived at by Hume or Kant or Spencer.

Transcendentalism as a method is a retreat to the subjective sphere, "a systematic subjectivism [WD, p. 193]" from which the return to the "external world" is to be made by means of a recognition of the way in which the mind's perspectives, categories, and ideas enter into the interpretations of that world. This method is employed in *Reason in Common Sense* where Santayana, following the "English psychologists" (though disowning sympathy for their "malicious attempt" to disintegrate faith in a natural world), attempts to reconstruct the manner in which the world comes to be known by a growing intelligence. Starting with an antecedent belief in the independent existence of the natural world, he would show how the dreaming mind, in the process of its being disciplined, gradually comes upon a discovery of natural objects.

Yet the naturalistic belief with which Santayana starts, and which persists throughout as an underlying assumption, is one that is not warranted by the manner in which that growing experience is construed. For that experience is wholly constituted of the mind's ideas, of its sensations, images, and thoughts. Nature and the world of existing substances become either "mental figments," constructs of these materials of subjective experience (something which Santayana later was himself to denounce as psychologism) or hidden realities, objects which these psychic states represent but "do not know." As an example of the former interpretation, consider the following passages:

A reality is a term of discourse based on a psychic complex of memories, associations, and expectations, but constituted in its ideal independence by the assertive energy of thought. An appearance is a passing sensation, recognized as belonging to that group of which the object itself is the ideal representative, and accordingly regarded as a manifestation of that object [LR, I, 82]; To discover a physical object is to pack in the same part of space, and fuse in one complex body, primary data like coloured form and tangible surface [ibid., p. 162]; [and finally] When you distinguish your sensations from their cause and laugh at the idealist (as this kind of sceptic is called) who says that chairs and tables exist only in your mind, you are treating a figment of reason as a deeper and truer thing than the moments of life whose blind experience that reason has come to illumine [ibid., p. 80].

Realities become terms of discourse, objects become constructs of psychic states, causes become figments of reason. Yet even if Santayana would escape from this Berkeleyan manner of speaking, he could but find himself in the arms of Locke. For that to which our ideas refer, if they themselves are not the sole constituents of reality, is an external material world, which indeed is taken as generating those ideas, but whose essence those ideas cannot disclose. The world is a hidden material engine, "the only possible object and theme of our knowledge," yet "something we cannot know [LR, I, 76]"; the intrinsic essence of matter [is] unknown [RM, p. vi]."

Santayana's analysis of sensation and perception in relation to the knowledge-situation reveals his essential kinship with the British empiricists. For him, as for them, sense-experience occupies a double status. On the one hand, the flux of sensations and the mass of particular observations forming the raw material from which the enterprise of science takes its start, are related to that enterprise as the natural is to the ideal. Immediate observations receive meaning when interpreted in terms of a structure or mechanism which thought discloses in nature. Knowledge is not pure, immediate, sensuous experience:

it is a salutation, not an embrace. It is an advance on sensation precisely because it is representative. The terms or goals of thought have for their function to subtend long tracts of sensuous experience, to be ideal links between fact and fact, invisible wires behind the scenes, threads along which inference may run in making the phenomena intelligible and controllable [LR, I, 77].

Knowledge, by which is thus meant a disclosure of the structures of natural forces, is indeed based upon an immediate acquaintance with the sensible forms which experience affords. Yet it is an advance upon such acquaintance with forms in that it goes beyond their mere presence to sense and reveals their systematic or intelligible connections in nature. Both the materials supplied by observation and the meaning revealed by intelligence are necessary. The latter supervenes upon the former, but in so supervening does not render its basis something that can be dismissed as being illusory or unnecessary. The empirical factor in knowledge is the ineradicable and only legitimate groundwork for the rational analysis of science.

Santayana, however, in common with the British empiricists, interprets sense-experience not only from the point of view of a sound observationalism but also from the point of view of a subjectivism which makes of experience an illusory screen of appearances hiding the inner essences of objects which that experience represents. Forms of sense are inadequate as means for disclosing the inner machinery that controls the movement of things. They are imaginative and pictorial fictions (cf. LR, V, 78–85). Instead of retaining sense-experience as the basis for all trustworthy knowledge, such experience is rejected in favor of an insight into the hidden mechanisms of objects, an insight revealing the real and efficacious structure of these mechanisms.

In *Reason in Science* Santayana, like Locke, is assured of the existence and possible knowledge of such a structure. Yet curiously enough, it is a knowledge which is to be obtained by means of further perception. "Science . . . passes . . . beyond the dreamlike unities and cadences which sense discloses: only, as science aims at controlling its speculation by experiment, the hidden reality it discloses is exactly like what sense perceives, though on a different scale [LR, V, 84–85]." Yet why organs of sensation should be more trustworthy on different scales of minuteness or magnitude, if they are throughout infected with a fictional character, is something which Santayana at this point does not explain. If ordinary perception is illusory, there can be no improvement when the organs or instruments of perception are refined, since it is the entire process of perception, rather than any refinement in its conditions or expression, that is taken to be infected with subjectivity. That Santayana does not, in these earlier discussions, wholly adopt this position with respect to the fictional character of experience, but rather alternates it with a realistic analysis must, of course, be recognized. In fact, one would be tempted to overlook his adoption of the language of psychological subjectivism as merely a possibly convenient manner of speaking, and as not implying the metaphysical consequences which its serious use would entail, were it not for the fact that the later volumes explicitly emphasize and bring to the foreground the suggestions of such a method and language as intermittently appear in *The Life of Reason*.

In *Scepticism and Animal Faith* the transcendental method and the agnostic conclusions are frankly adopted by Santayana. The latter is the only escape from the solipsism of the present moment and the assertionless intuition of essences to which the transcendental method ultimately leads. With unfailing, relentless logic, Santayana shows, in the first half of that volume, how, once the skeptical solvent has begun its work, all knowledge of natural objects becomes something we cannot defend. All that remains to us is the immediate intuition of a given essence. The return to the natural world is made at the bidding of our animal faith, which persuades us we live in a world composed of interacting natural substances. Knowledge, then, becomes a species of animal faith using the essences present to intuition as symbols for those external forces that intrude themselves within our experience by the "shocks" and imperiousness of their presence.

Yet all we can have, at most, is a practical adjustment to these facts of existence; rarely, if ever, do we acquire an insight into their inmost real and intelligible structure. Experience is primarily imaginative and poetical. From ordinary perceptions to the highest flights of poetry, religion, and even science, the terms employed are essentially "dream-images." Experience is a normal madness that moves in a conventional (or fictional) world of phenomena, the real world of substances being seen always as dressed up in the garments which intuition creates. "In the routine of animal life, an appearance may be normal or abnormal, and animal faith or practical intellect may interpret it in a way practically right or wrong; but in itself every appearance, just because it is an appearance, is an illusion [SAF, p. 63]." All our descriptions and ideas are but symbols for the underlying rumble of the realm of matter. These ideas make the world familiar to us as a nickname does an object, except—and this is an important qualification—that the nickname and the object do not lie in the same plane of reality. Ideas, for Santayana, are symbolic of that which lies beyond them; they are not the objects of knowledge but the means whereby such objects are signified. In themselves these essences or ideas possess their own aesthetic or logical being, but for ordinary practical or cognitive purposes one does not stop to regard these. Rather they are used in designating, identifying, and referring to objects intended by animal faith and met with in the course of action. And such animal faith is needed because ultimately, for Santayana as for Locke, these ideas are opaque. If the only data of experience are essences, not objects, and yet if it is to objects to which we refer, we need some ground for justifying that reference. And this ground is recognized as an irrational, instinctive faith in the actual presence of those objects.

Signs for Santayana are essentially names, qualitatively unlike their objects. To believe that signs or aesthetic data constitute the object is idolatry. Yet what ultimately leads to agnosticism on this theory of knowledge is, not that knowledge is construed as symbolic, referential or mediate, all of which it undeniably is, but rather the fact that the order of signs and the order of objects are placed in two diverse realms. Knowledge, then, is made to consist of a transitive leap from the realm of essence to the realm of matter, instead of being made to consist of a transition within one context from symbol to fact, from theory to that which it designates in experience or to that which is identified by perception. In this latter view, which Santayana himself at one time suggested, we have knowledge when we verify what is asserted by some judgment (which is a symbol) through intent in dialectic or by experiment in physics.

For in general, as we are told in *The Life of Reason*, the success of the rational life depends on the effective symbolic representation by reason of the conditions and interests of human activity. This continuous and relevant symbolic functioning is wholly naturalistic, in that both ideas and their objects, like a map and the countryside it represents, like smoke and fire, like the child's outstretched hand and the moon it points to, like theory and perceived fact, all fall within a single total sphere of objects and events. The objects of symbolic designation are not things-in-themselves— hidden realities unknown in their true essence. They are, rather, within the actual process of experience, the continually verified and verifiable objects or thoughts of daily living (cf. OS, p. 115; LR, V, 317–18).

Appearances are the qualities of reality, else realities would be without place, time, character, or interrelation. . . . Appearances define the constituent elements of . . . reality, which could not be better known than through their means [LR, V, 165–66].

For a realistic view, then, as contrasted with an agnostic view, there is no belief in an unknowable object. Rather, there is a judgment with respect to an object, this object being constituted of a concretion or residuum of verified qualities and relations. In such a view, science "contains the sum total of our rational convictions and gives us the only picture of reality on which we should care to dwell [LR, V, 319]." But from the point of view of an agnosticism such as his later writings develop, Santayana is forced to conclude that "science, when it is more than the gossip of adventure or of experiment, yields practical assurances couched in symbolic terms, but no ultimate insight [STTMP, p. 79]."

Ontologic dualism.—The lack of this ultimate insight, which even science can never avoid, has its consequences for a theory of nature and morals. It makes an honest cosmology, if not impossible (since our belief in nature is taken to be grounded in an instinctive animal faith), then at least meager. And it makes of the life of reason, which from this point of view is described in Spencerian language as an "adjustment of inner to outer relations [cf. BHMO, p. 249]," a matter of practical necessity, the price that must be paid for existing at all, rather than the seat of all ultimate values. The latter is now to be found in a spiritual life no longer devoted to anxiety about existence, but to the care-free imaginative and aesthetic intuition of essences. These essences are taken as forming no part of nature (since the realm of matter is entirely distinct from the realm of essence) and as no longer possessing a purely practical, symbolic, or referential rôle in guiding action or thought.

In some of Santayana's writings, especially *The Life of Reason,* the ultimate agnosticism to which the transcendental method leads, is not entirely insisted upon. For to science alone he there gives the office of revealing the truth about nature, although the effect of this revelation upon the other phases of the life of reason is to render them illusory. For the basic reality of nature in the light of scientific analysis becomes exhausted in its mechanical framework, and all the fruits of this mechanism become but ideal and redundant elements, in no way implicated in this mechanical structure. The findings of mechanical science become converted into the principles of a mechanistic metaphysics, in which life, mind, value, and the products of consciousness in general are set over against the "engine" of nature, as appearance is to reality. Mind becomes the "erratic residue of existence."

As material objects, making a single system which fills space and evolves in time, are conceived by abstraction from the flux of sensuous experience, so, *pari passu,* the rest of experience, with all its other outgrowths and concretions, falls out with the physical world and forms the sphere of mind, the sphere of memory, fancy, and the passions. . . . As attention awakes and discrimination, practically inspired, grows firm and stable, irrelevant qualities are stripped off, and the mechanical process, the efficacious infallible order, is clearly disclosed beneath. Meantime the incidental effects, the "secondary qualities," are relegated to a personal inconsequential region; they constitute the realm of appearance, the realm of mind [LR, I, 124–26].

Whereas, as we have seen, in the genuinely naturalistic portions of his metaphysics, Santayana avoids a sharp breach between the mental and the physical, the ideal and the mechanical, viewing them rather in Aristotelian terms as different levels of activity and interaction, equally real though qualitatively diverse, in statements such as the above and in many other passages of like import he follows the Cartesian tradition of modern philosophy in its sharp separation of these facts into totally distinct realms. Santayana's own attempt at reconstructing a union between the mental and the physical follows the system generally known as epiphenomenalism; the body is the "lyric cry," "register," "accompaniment," and "celebration" of bodily activities. Yet this attempted reconciliation, like all other suggested solutions to a fictitious problem, is ultimately unsuccessful. One cannot deny all instrumental efficacy to thought ("thought is nature's concomitant expression or entelechy, never one of her instruments [LR, I, 223; cf. LR, I, 213 ff.]"), and still maintain that "man's rational life consists in those moments in which reflection not only occurs but proves efficacious [LR, I, 2]."

Santayana's epiphenomenalism is inconsistent with the practical rôle he assigns to intelligence in the life of reason. That it does possess such a rôle follows easily enough from the naturalistic premise that there is an order of substances, qualities, and powers constituted in various ways, possessed of varying abilities to enter into mechanical, animate, cognitive, and consciously transformative relations with one another. It is in terms of such a premise that the morality of the life of reason itself is made intelligible. For reason is a power which man, as a natural substance, possesses, which enables him to look ahead and back, to direct his activities in accordance with his ability to modify impulse, and to control, within limits, the course of natural events. But if we draw a sharp line between the mechanical and the mental, putting all efficacy in the former, then thought becomes truly impotent and redundant in the march of events, a helpless spectator having no practical control over the instruments and conditions of its activity. For "The mind at best vaguely forecasts the result of action . . . but this premonition is itself the sense of a process already present and betrays the tendency at work; it can obviously give no aid or direction to the unknown mechanical process that produced it and that must realise its own prophecy, if that prophecy is to be realised at all [LR, I, 214–15]."

The consequences of imputing reality to the findings of mechanical science, while relegating the mind and all its works to the sphere of appearance, are such that they disturb the naturalism of Santayana's philosophy and the humanism which that philosophy has done so much to place in its proper setting. In his later writings Santayana develops the full implications of his transcendental method and realizes that not even science can ultimately disclose the truth about nature. The terms of science, while more accurate and practically reliable than those of religion or common sense, are nevertheless like them essentially symbolic and poetic. They do not suffice to disclose the inner essence of matter. One cannot, therefore, assert even that the mechanisms discovered by science constitute the actual structures of events and substances.

The realm of matter can never be disclosed either to hypothesis or to sensation in its presumable inmost structure and ultimate extent: the garment of appearance must always fit it loosely and drape it in alien folds, because appearance is essentially an adaptation of facts to the scale and faculty of the observer [RE, p. xii]. The question is which imaginative system you will trust. My matured conclusion has been that no system is to be trusted, not even that of science in any literal or pictorial sense; but all systems may be used and, up to a certain point, trusted as symbols [BHMO, pp. 243–44].

In the later writings, as a result, the form of ontologic dualism that emerges is to be construed differently from that which it has in the writings of the middle period. The antithesis is now to be found in the sharp separation of the realm of matter from the realm of essence.

In terms of our knowledge of and moral concerns with these realms, the distinction lies between that which is hidden from our direct insight into its structure and that which is entirely obvious and the direct theme of intuition and discourse; between that which is the scene of all action, generation, doubt, and contingency, and that which is the abode of eternal, certain, and universal forms. The combination of both of these sets of characterizations yields an ontology that leans equally on Locke and Plato. Santayana transforms the ideas that intervene as a screen between the spirit and the external world into a realm of timeless universals, distinct from the realm of evanescent and contingent flux of material particulars encountered in action.

The result is a form of ontologic dualism that is metaphysical in precisely the sense which Santayana would avoid. For this dualism results from transferring the foreground of sensuous, imaginative, and intellectual experience into the eternal background of nature itself:

A foreground [Santàyana tells us] is by definition relative to some chosen point of view, to the station assumed in the midst of nature by some creature tethered by fortune to a particular time and place.

If such a foreground becomes dominant in a philosophy naturalism is abandoned. Some local perspective or some casual interest is set up in the place of universal nature or behind it, or before it, so that all the rest of nature is reputed to be intrinsically remote or dubious or merely ideal. This dominance of the foreground has always been the source of metaphysics; and the metaphysics has varied according as the foreground has been occupied by language or fancy or logical or sceptical self-consciousness or religious rapture or moral ambition [OS, pp. 223–24].

The realm of essence as it figures in Santayana's own system occupies a metaphysical status in two respects: it is set up before nature, in so far as it functions in knowledge as a screen hiding the realm of matter from possible insight into its structure; and it is set up behind nature, in so far as it constitutes a realm of eternal objects having prior and independent being with respect to material objects. The transference of the latter sort raises to ontologic dignity and independence something which in reality is but the natural product of a form of experience realized within the confines of natural existence itself.

Essences or ideas, which in Santayana's earlier writings were interpreted from a thoroughly naturalistic point of view as descriptions, principles, or foreshadowings of natural events, assume in the later writings a status similar to that assigned them in all forms of Platonism. Plato hypostatized moral and intellectual ideals, whereas for Santayana the realm of essence includes every possible form, every conceivable, sensible, or imaginable quality or relation. Yet the status of the two from a naturalistic point of view is the same. They both constitute an illegitimate conversion of certain selected aspects of experience into the essence of reality itself. Santayana's criticism of Platonism in *The Life of Reason,* if we make the necessary qualifications concerning the scope of the Ideas in his own system as compared with that which they have in Plato, might be repeated almost verbatim as applying to his own descriptions of the realm of essence.

Plato saw in concretions in discourse the true elements of being. Definable meanings, being the terms of thought, must also, he fancied, be the constituents of reality. And with that directness and audacity which was possible to the ancients . . . he set up these terms of discourse, like the Pythagorean numbers, for absolute and eternal entities, existing before all things, revealed in all things, giving the cosmic artificer his models and the creature his goal. . . . The radical fault of rationalism . . . is its denial of its own basis and its refusal to occupy its due place in the world, an ignorant fear of being invalidated by its history and dishonoured, as it were, if its ancestry is hinted at [LR, I, 193, 200].

The motivation for setting up the realm of essence as against the realm of matter is to be found partly in the failure of the theory of knowledge, as we find it in *Scepticism and Animal Faith,* to make ideas function as effective instruments in disclosing the traits of nature; and partly in the desire, reflected in the post-rational aspects of the spiritual life, to escape from the contingency of natural existence. For it is in the realm of essence that the spirit, according to Santayana, finds its salvation. The eternity, certainty, and impartiality of essences bestow their qualities on human experience in its contemplative moments. The realm of matter, while providing the occasions for such contemplation, is nevertheless in its very existence and arbitrary determinations an irrational and absurd flux of events. Even the realm of truth, that portion of infinite possibility that happens to be embodied in matter, is but a tragic segment of the entire realm of essence. For the philosopher, intent upon viewing things in the light of the eternal and the infinite, the realm of essence provides the ultimate standard and goal of insight.

The post-rational aspects of the spiritual life find their corollaries in the transcendental or mystical dissolution of knowledge into the intuition of essences, and in the metaphysical preëminence possessed by the realm of essence over the domains of matter and truth. However, before we turn to a consideration of the spiritual life in its relation to these matters, it will be well to consider the earlier version of Santayana's moral philosophy, as expressed in *The Life of Reason,* in order that we may see to what extent the spiritual life is an extension of or a refined emphasis upon certain of the themes treated there, and to what extent, in being a post-rational system, it is actually a departure from rational ethics.

II

THE LIFE OF REASON

Meanings of "the life of reason."—What precisely are we to understand by the phrase "the life of reason"? A general and provisionally abstract definition might be given by saying that it is a type of human conduct in which "everything ideal has a natural basis and everything natural an ideal development[LR, I, 21]." Yet this definition, now classic, is of little value until we appreciate the manifold contexts by which it may be illustrated and the specific senses in which its terms may be understood. For does the "life of reason" describe the general career or the historical progress of mankind in rationalizing and perfecting its various institutions, or is it, rather, a name for the historically unrealized yet ethically definable composite ideal of all its possible perfections? Does the life of reason define the ethics of personal or individual conduct as well as that of society or the race as a whole? Does the conception of the life of reason depend for illustrative content upon the inclusion of specific values, or can it also be defined in terms of general principles apart from a reference to particular values?

The fact is that Santayana uses the phrase in each of the above senses and in each of these several contexts, with the result that it takes on a somewhat special meaning as we go from one to the other. We may recognize, therefore, at least three characteristic ways in which the life of reason may be discussed, depending upon whether the reference is to human history or civilization and its institutions of society, art, religion, and science; or to individual conduct and the mode of functioning of specific interests, activities, or impulses; or finally, to a theory of moral value in which the essential principles involved in the analysis of the two previous specific realms—human nature in the sense of the race and its characteristic institutions, and human nature in the sense of the collection of specific traits or interests summed up in a single life—are generalized and made to constitute an abstract though specific theory of the good life.

The Life of Reason as an analysis of the various aspects, subdivisions, historical manifestations, and possible ideal values of institutions such as society, art, religion, and science, constitutes a philosophy of history and civilization. The employment of the terms "natural condition" and "ideal development" in this context possesses a double significance. On the one hand, in so far as the emphasis is a genetic one, treating of the dynamic career or growth process of any human activity, these terms signify respectively the initially crude and finally perfected phases of that career or process. On the other hand, in so far as the analysis is a moral one of levels or gradations of values statically or organically conceived, so to speak, then these terms are analogous to the Aristotelian principles of matter and form, natural conditions constituting the means or efficacious foundation for a supervening ideal employment of those means. In the one case *The Life of Reason* constitutes an ethical appraisal of history and a forecast of its possible development; in the other it defines a philosophy of civilization, estimating the relative moral values, functions, and status of institutions and their elements in the architectonic of a rational culture.

The genetic emphasis makes of the life of reason a history

of progress, an account of the various phases involved in rationalizing or perfecting characteristic human impulses and institutions. The term "life," when this signifies the type of behavior or trope proper to organic beings, denotes a span or career of activities from birth to death, as well as the fact of active participation in or interaction with the natural environment at any cross section or moment of the career. Taken in the first of these senses the term "life" becomes in the case of the individual his biography and in the case of humanity or any of its institutions, a synonym for its history.

A distinction must be made, however, between history or evolution on the one hand and moral progress on the other, for whereas the former is always a fact, illustrating the inevitable flux of existence, the latter appears only when there is a discernible, continuous change for the better; far from being inevitable, it is but the happy achievement of some selected ideal. Failure to make this distinction leaves us with a stultifying belief in the inevitability of progress. Yet nothing would do greater violence to our moral estimation of history. "Modern Greece is not exactly the crown of ancient Hellas." To identify moral growth with historical change, no matter in what manner the latter occurs, forces the obliteration of all distinction between the actual and the ideal, and every change, no matter how evil, must necessarily be reckoned as a good. Santayana emphatically rejects the belief in the inevitability of progress, as a superstition on a par with the belief in Providence, Fate, or the magical efficacy of the number three. The life of reason is a general name, therefore, for the sum total of those phases of human history in which can be noted a definite progress toward ideal perfections in science, art, religion, and society. At times Santayana, however, uses the phrase not only for the genetic process but also for the very ideal in terms of which the progress is to be measured. It then signifies not the career of reason but rational activity or living, the composite possible ideal achievements that define the goal of civilization.

Of the many discussions in *The Life of Reason* that may be taken to illustrate its genetic emphasis, we might select that in which Santayana traces an ideal development in religious life from its primitive forms of magic, superstition, and mythology, to its rationalized forms of piety and spirituality. In superstition, the mind, in its first tentative gropings at understanding the causal processes of nature, develops a misguided belief in miracles—misguided in so far as causes are confused with their purposes or results. Thus if one, in drinking the water of Lourdes were to believe the cure (if there is one) to come about as a result of faith and prayers, he would be converting what is an ideal result into an efficient cause. From the point of view of science, which perceives the efficacious and non-morally determined order of natural events, such belief in the miraculous is sheer superstition.

In magic, sacrifice, and prayer—representing the attempts to control natural forces, and in mythology—the attempt to understand them, the crude religious response, when relying on these means literally, likewise fails, in so far as it usurps the only effective techniques of technology and pure science. The emotions of fear and need surrounding the momentous crises of life in disease, tempest, death, hunger, and victory, arouse the attempt to control these facts by invoking the aid of natural or supernatural forces through such means as magical rites, supplication, and sacrifice. These means are abortive to the extent that there is no clear understanding of the effective mechanisms that would, in fact, bring about or prevent the occurrence of the phenomena. In mythology the primitive religious mind uses psychic and morally dramatic categories in interpreting nature and its significance for human experience. Taken literally such myths, constructed to justify magic, are regarded as affording us information about the conditions, powers, and outcome of cosmic or human history. In them gods and demons are believed to direct and control natural events. As myths, they are at the opposite pole from science, since the latter defines and explores only such facts as are experimentally and perceptually verifiable. Dante, for example, gave us "bad cosmography and worse history[LR, III, 56]." Yet taken for what they are rationally worth, myths constitute genuine poetic expressions of moral ideals. Gods become symbols for human ideals, not metaphysical powers.

And in general rational religion, shorn of its misdirected attempts to replace science and technology, is seen to consist of a comprehensive poetic expression of moral idealism, reflected in the attitudes of piety and spirituality. When rightfully understood, the symbols it employs are the poetry of reverence and aspiration, the imaginative representation of the sources and ideals of human experience in a natural world. Piety consists of loyalty to necessary conditions, a sentiment of reverent gratitude addressed to those conditions on which the very existence of a given life depends, "parents first, then family, ancestors, and country; finally, humanity at large and the whole natural cosmos [LR, III, 179]." Spirituality consists of devotion to ideal ends, as these are limited in their scope by the natural confines of our earthly existence. To be spiritual, as Santayana defines it in this early analysis, is not to renounce life and the moral values it makes possible. On the contrary, it is to accept the irrationally given, to imaginatively elaborate the possible values thereof, and to make of its material a rationally integrated whole.

In general, then, as a philosophy of development the enterprise of *The Life of Reason* involves a double reference, to history and to ethics. The general procedure is to gather from the facts of history and anthropology a knowledge of characteristic human activities, and in the light of a careful examination of their possible ideal values, as determined by intelligent criticism, to indicate what is or might be their order of growth. If there can be discovered in history an actual transition from an irrational or crude state of some mode of life to its ideal form, that history may be said to illustrate a moral progress. The development of science in the Western World is an obvious illustration of such progress in history.

On the other hand, while the ethical analysis takes as its field the characteristic institutions of man's history, it by no means follows that the end of that analysis, the discrimination of the possible ideals of such institutions, is thereby converted into a report of their actual embodiment in past history or a prediction of their necessary enactment in the future. The ethical analysis begins with an examination of historical fact, but the end of such analysis is in no case the efficient cause of the historical series or its necessarily actual end. The ideal conceived becomes rather a means for estimating the course of actual events, in the attempt to discover to what extent the ideal has been approached or embodied. The definition of the life of reason as an ideal is a matter of prospective ethics; the extent to which the career of man illustrates progress in achieving that ideal is a matter of history and retrospective politics (cf. LR, V, 58). Yet each analysis involves the other, since on the one hand the definition of the life of reason as an ideal requires the facts of history as its natural basis; and, on the other, the discrimination of the history of progress or the developing life of reason from the total and infinitely complex series of all historical events likewise demands the conscious use of a selected norm or ideal standard. The presentation of *The Life of Reason,* therefore, is at once historical and normative. It involves both memory and moral judgment (cf. LR, I, 2). Without the former the ethics would be empty and without the latter the history would be blind and uninstructive.

Santayana's analyses, however, as we have said, are not entirely of a genetic character, tracing the transformation of an activity from its primitive, irrational stages to its perfected or ideal ones. His use of the terms "natural basis" and "ideal development" bear the added meanings relevant to a discussion of comparative values or gradation of interests, in which we may say that natural conditions constitute subordinate elements in the organic composition of more inclusive and representative ends. It is in this context that we may speak of natural society as constituting the basis for free and ideal society, physics for ethics, piety for spirituality, and industrial art for fine art. In each case the activity represented by the second of these terms constitutes the ideal employment and organization of the materials supplied by the first.

Ultimately the race is the total of its individual members, and the values of its institutions are those that can be enjoyed and shared by individual men. Happiness, the goal of all ethical inquiry, can be predicated in the end only of what is attained in a single life. "The only natural unit in morals is the individual man, because no other natural unit is synthesized by nature herself into a living spirit [GTB, p. 54]." The concept of the life of reason, when applied thus to the realm of personal conduct, denotes the conditions and principles of behavior that define the perfections possible to each man. This is a type of life grounded in the specific natural endowments or faculties of the individual, resulting from intelligent self-knowledge, and embodying the perfections possible to such an individual.

As used in the most general sense of all, the life of reason depends for its meaning on the definition of general concepts such as natural impulse, intelligence, perfection, and harmony. This general use of the phrase appears in statements such as the following:

The Life of Reason [is] a name for that part of experience which perceives and pursues ideals—all conduct so controlled and all sense so interpreted as to perfect natural happiness[LR, I, 3]. In the Life of Reason, if it were brought to perfection, intelligence would be at once the universal method of practice and its continual reward [LR, I, 5]. The Life of Reason is the happy marriage of two elements—impulse and ideation—which if wholly divorced would reduce man to a brute or to a maniac[LR, I, 6]. The Life of Reason, being the sphere of all human art, is man's imitation of divinity [LR, I, 7; cf. LR, IV, 208].

What, may we ask, is the context to which a discussion of such a general and abstract ideal is relevant? To what subject does it belong, whose ideal is being described? On this general level of discourse the answer must be that it applies to man as a natural species. It defines a general ideal, the essential structure of which is capable of accommodating a variety of illustrative materials gathered both from the history of culture and from the conduct of individuals.

With respect to this abstract conception of the life of reason, three basic categories may be taken as defining its essential structure: natural conditions, intelligence, and the ideal. "The forces at play in this drama are first, the primary impulses and functions represented by elementary values; second the thin network of signals and responses by which those functions are woven into a total organ, represented by discursive thought and all secondary mental figments, and third, the equilibrium and total power of that new organism in action represented by the ideal[LR, III, 199]." Or again, "the life of reason [is] empirical in its basis and rational in its method, its substance impulse and its end happiness[LR, V, 290]."

These three principles, in turn, call attention to three important sets of questions in moral theory: first, what are the given facts of man's actual behavior, historically, biologically, culturally? Second, what in the light of these existent facts are the morally desirable and ideal forms of activity, what the genuine ends of conduct? And third, how is the transition from the actual to the ideal to be made, and what rôle does intelligence or practical reason play in this development? These three phases delimit a unified situation and for the life of reason are mutually interdependent.

We propose in the remainder of this chapter to examine some of Santayana's leading ideas on each of these topics, as these may be gathered from his various writings.

Natural conditions.—A definition of the life of reason involves a recognition of the specific natural conditions of that life. A naturalistic approach points to the status of human life within the larger context of nature; it emphasizes the inescapable givenness of natural events and the materials of conduct; it defines the fundamental place of interest, impulse, and habit as the grounds of moral preference and judgment; it calls attention to elements both of constancy and variability in moral systems; and, finally, it exhibits the locus of moral problems by pointing to their origin and initial setting. This last point calls attention to the fact that a recognition of the natural conditions of the life of reason is but the beginning and not the end of moral inquiry and endeavor.

The first effect of a naturalistic outlook upon a consideration of human affairs is the recognition of the proper place of human life in its larger setting of nature, in the general dynamic continuity and evolution of natural existence. Man as a portion of the natural flux inhabits this realm together with the stars, the plants, and the other animals; his existence is as much an illustration of nature's productivity as theirs (cf. LR, I, 277, 288–89).

Since human nature is no exception in the natural history of the world, nature exists as little for its sake as for the sake of anything else, and as much. Of course there is a difference between man and the other natural products—his possession of intelligence and a conscious pursuit of ends. These are unique qualities and they have important and novel consequences, for by them man can intelligently turn nature to his own uses. Since life is not a supernatural event either in its origin or in its significance, the natural materials of man's own given structure and nature's constitution exhaustively define the setting for the operation of intelligence. Living well in such a setting is a natural art, the complete and perfect functioning of all human potentialities, not, as another tradition would have it, the result of blindly following authoritatively imposed and supposedly supernatural commands.

Historically the immediate consequence of a liberation of man from the dominion of supernatural importance and significance was a sense of freedom from the bonds of tradition or authority. Naturalism in ethics has therefore often come to mean a denial of moral discipline and organized liberty. Such, says Santayana, was the youthful naturalism of the nineteenth-century positivists(LR, I, 9–10). In discarding the entire machinery of traditional religion and its symbolic expression of the ideal life, this naturalism neglected to put anything in its place. To a complete naturalism, however, the nature of man, with his diversified functions, contains within itself the principles of all morality. Naturalism, when full-grown and aware not only of the legitimacy but of the importance of a moral idealism built on this basis, is sufficient unto itself (cf. GTB, p. 51).

It is this insistence on the primacy of the context and the setting of nature for moral idealism, where the latter constitutes one part or aspect of natural existence as embodied in the human sphere, that sharply separates Santayana from those metaphysical idealists of the German school, who invert the relation by viewing the faculty and energy of idealization as the central and universal power in the universe at large. Nature ultimately envelops and conditions the phenomena of consciousness and valuation, not the other way around.

It is a fault of idealists to misrepresent idealism, because they do not view it as a part of the world. Idealism *is* a part of the world, a small and dependent part—even in the life of men. This fact is nothing against idealism taken as a moral energy, as a faculty of idealization and a habit of living in the familiar presence of an image of what would, in everything, be best [TPP, p. 61].

Santayana is a follower of Aristotle and Lucretius, not of Fichte and Hegel.

A naturalistic approach to morality also involves the acceptance of given facts of behavior and the natural order of cosmological occurrences as ultimately inescapable. Just as in another context the fear of the Lord is the beginning of wisdom, so in the context of rational morality the beginning of wisdom is, not fear, but a candid inspection of the given and an intelligent analysis of the opportunities it affords (cf. RM, pp. 205–6). An analysis of the given reveals that the moral attitude does not have a moral ground; the judgments of conscience or the rational evaluation and estimation of goods are conditioned by what is not moral, by what is itself ultimately, in other words, not amenable to voluntary choice (cf. GTB, p. 54). Morality, the principle of all choices in taste, faith, and allegiance has its natural basis in an inherited animal and social structure. Since this structure, however, is in constant interaction with a natural environment, the latter too presents certain given habits or laws of action that serve to define the limits for human activity. The given is irrationally given; though there may be dispute or preference from a moral point of view about what might be done with the given, there can be no escape from the given in some form or other, since in the very act of pronouncement of preference or dispute, there is a given element present, that of desire at the bottom of the judgment and that of the materials about which the judgment is made. The fact of will, the given of behavior, and the fact of mechanism, the given of natural knowledge, cannot be escaped. The given material organs of man's body and of society, and the given material forces and structure of inorganic nature with which these organs are in constant external relations must be the starting point of any serious moral philosophy.

This recognition of the naturally given is at once sad and enlightening; it demands an ultimate surrender but it also affords an opportunity for rational endeavor. The aversion to mechanism is partly natural.

Like the aversion to death, to old age, to labour, it is called forth by man's natural situation in a world which was not made for him, but in which he grew. That the efficacious structure of things should not be intentionally spectacular nor poetical, that its units should not be terms in common discourse, nor its laws quite like the logic of passion, is of course a hard lesson to learn. The learning, however —not to speak of its incidental delights—is so extraordinarily good for people that only with that instruction and the blessed renunciation it brings can clearness, dignity, or virility enter their minds [LR, V, 85–86; cf. LR, I, 191; LP, p. 165; LR, IV, 169].

The need for resignation to the ultimate natural basis of things does not mean that such an order is either wholly good or wholly evil. The first would be optimistic pantheism, the second pessimistic fatalism; both are incompatible with a theory of the order of the universe which sees such an order as in itself morally neutral, and as existing for good or ill only in so far as man's interaction with its mechanism results in the one or the other (cf. BHMO, pp. 246–47; LR, V, 216). Santayana's conception of nature is in this respect similar to Spinoza's; both stress on its morally neutral quality. For nature neither condemns nor rejects any particular existence, inasmuch as such existence is the inevitable fruit of its productivity. Our own standards are relative to our needs and

purposes, but these cannot be subordinated in their claims to
the will of some higher authority, since there is no such
authority. Nature has no plan and illustrates no moral intent.

Mechanism, therefore, should be judged by its fruits. It is
not only the inevitable actuality of a given order of facts that
must be recognized by an ethics based on naturalistic premises, but also the ideal possibilities that can be produced by
an intelligent manipulation of those same mechanisms.
Though the world is mechanically efficacious, it is not merely
that, and in the case of human civilization it flowers into a type
of natural existence where value, rationality, and a conscious
idealization of experience play a thoroughly intelligible rôle.

A closer inspection of human nature reveals that it is "a
fundamental essence, a collection of activities with determinate limits, relations and ideals." Since the essence of man's
moral life is the fixation of interests or the pursuit of ideals,
it is necessary, in order to understand this essence, to discover
its immediate natural ground. When employed in this connection, the principle of naturalism points to the primacy of interest and habit as the original motivating forces of behavior
and the initial determinants of value. "Values spring from the
immediate and inexplicable reaction of vital impulse, and
from the irrational part of our nature [SB, p. 19]."

In impulse we have the stuff of morals; the substance of
life is the multifarious complex of its desires and its needs.
Santayana uses the term "impulse" sometimes in a narrower
and sometimes in a broader sense. In the broader sense of
the term, impulse means not only what it ordinarily connotes
—the biological expression of some bodily or organic tension
—but also the fact of interest on every level of life. It then
includes not only such things as the drives of hunger and sex,
but various economic, parental, or political interests of social
life, as well as the interests of imagination and reflection as
these express themselves in science, art, and religion. Santa-

yana thus follows Aristotle in recognizing desire as the single, ultimate cause of activity, a cause operating on all levels of animate behavior. A study of man's conduct therefore becomes mainly an inquiry into the nature of his desires, how they arise, how they are transformed and rationalized, and how they find their way into action.

In the narrower sense of the term "natural impulse," reference is made to what is sometimes called the "lower" or irrational side of human nature, in contrast to the "higher" or rational side, as the latter is expressed in the imaginative and reflective activities of religion, art, and science. In that case it includes the purely organic or wholly automatic and irrational forces operating in the individual or in society. In the individual these impulses, such as the food or sex impulses, appear recurrently and assume the form of habits. In the case of society, various mores, primitive social instincts (such as the parental), and differences of individual, economic, and racial endowment, springing up irrationally, constitute the basis from which any idealizing or rationalizing efforts must take their start.

The doctrine of the primacy of impulse, therefore, where impulse may be momentary, intermittent, or habitual, signifies that in considering the grounds of the expression of value or the basis of ideal achievements, either in the case of the individual's activity or in the case of the experience of the race, reference must be made to prior determinations in the psychological constitution of the individual and to the deposits of historical antecedents and various types of social motivation in the race. To treat the alleged reasons for our actions as their primary ground is to commit the fallacy of intellectualism. Santayana follows Schopenhauer in recognizing the priority of will over the intellect. Reason and a conscious pursuit of ideals arise, in other words, in a life or in a society already possessing a modicum of organization and

already engaged in the business of satisfying needs and desires. A predetermined automatic organization of animal instincts and habits must be established in a life before one
can consciously discover its direction or plan and attempt its
greater perfection (cf. LR, II, 137, 174; V, 246; I, 40, 43,
277). We act, not because in acting we attain some good, rather
we attain some good because we already find ourselves acting.
It is not given to the individual nor to the race to debate Hamlet's question, since existence and a prior determination of
activity are things given and not asked for. "When once the
die is cast and we exist, so that Hamlet's question can be put
to us, the answer is already given; nature in forming us has
compelled us to prejudge the case[SE, p. 28)." When reason
is born and debating is possible, we already find ourselves
acting, and the only proper question is not whether it is
worth while to act, but only, given the fact of activity, how
this can be transformed so as to yield experiences that are
at once intrinsically valuable and satisfying.

The supervening interests of science, art, and religion, that
together constitute the "rational" side of human nature and
have as their function this transformation and rationalization
of experiences, are grounded in the irrational forces of individual or corporate behavior.

Reason could not exist or be conceived at all unless a material organism, personal or social lay beneath to give thought an occasion
and a point of view, and to give preference a direction. Things could
not be near or far, worse or better, unless a definite life were taken
as a standard, a life lodged somewhere in space and time. Reason is
a principle of order appearing in a subject-matter which in its sub-
sistence and quantity must be an irrational datum. Reason expresses
purpose, purpose expresses impulse, and impulse expresses a natural
body with self-equilibrating powers[LR, II, 137–38].

For example, the science of nutrition and the art of plowing
take their origin in the rudimentary need for food, and their
ideal value is determined by the continued existence of such

need. They may, it is true, develop their own ideals, so that to discover a perfect method of plowing or clearly to understand the chemistry of foods may be genuine goods, but they could never have arisen nor be ultimately justified unless they had this practical relevance to a recurrent animal need (cf. LR, II, 56). The series of interests on the various levels of rational life may thus be compared to a set of concentric circles in which each new level possesses its own boundaries and ends, yet is determined for its locus by each preceding level and by the core of given material faculties and habits. Morality, religion, art, and science express or protect ultimately basic animal passions, in the life of reason; they surround and extend them, but they do not get beyond them.

All interests of life, furthermore, both those which man possesses as his unique distinction from the brutes (the ability to represent the conditions and ideals of life, and to take practical steps in the light of that knowledge), and those which he possesses in common with the brutes (the various organic or purely biologic functions), are, in their original forms, crude and unenlightened. The interests that define the rational or conscious efforts of art, science, and religion not only are dependent for their material basis upon a core of wholly irrational bodily or social needs, but in their attempts to meet those needs and to clarify or improve the conditions and ends of life illustrate in themselves a development from a stage in which such attempts are "irrational" and wholly imperfect to a gradually emerging clarification of ideal methods and purposes. To contrast the tentative beginnings of barbaric religion and art, or primitive science and philosophy, with their more or less enlightened forms, illustrates this point. Rational interests constituting the special endowment of consciousness in man are themselves in their first appearances irrational, that is, at the opposite pole from their possible ideal employment. Intelligence and the process of idealization need to be applied to them no less than to wholly irrational or purely organic functions of man. Reason in art, religion, and science is the term applied to the method of the development of these from crude and imperfect forms of activity to ideal ones. And in general the process of growth in any phase of life is simply the development of the ideal out of the natural, the perfect out of the imperfect.

This leads immediately to another important aspect of a naturalistic approach to morals, namely that all values, goods, and ideals, are relative to given interests or desires. Santayana states this point succinctly in the *Sense of Beauty:*

there is no value apart from some appreciation of it, and no good apart from some preference of it before its absence or its opposite. In appreciation, in preference, lies the root and essence of all excellence. Or, as Spinoza clearly expresses it, we desire nothing because it is good, but it is good only because we desire it [*ibid.,* p. 18]. The desire for an object logically precedes and conditions whatever pleasures are enjoyed in its attainment [cf. LR, I, 223].

Values or goods, therefore, on this view are neither existentially unconditioned nor wholly independent of human experience. They are qualified experiences determined by the reaction of vital impulse and not objectively independent, since apart from such impulse they have no natural or intelligible status. To make values independent of human nature is to convert something which is essentially adjectival and relative into something substantive and absolute. In this direction lies mythology. Values are not objective in the sense of being a priori or antecedently real. They are objective only in so far as the whole situation of interest and its correlative value-object is objective, that is, an event taking place in the world. In short,

values presuppose living beings having a direction of development, and exerting themselves in it, so that good and evil may exist in reference to them. That the good should be relative to actual natures and simply their innate ideal, latent or realized, is essential to its being truly a good. Otherwise the term "good" would be an empty title applied to some existing object or force for no assignable reason [PSL, pp. 13–14].

While Santayana's general position with respect to the definition of the good or of value may thus be called a form of naturalistic relativism, it is at the same time perfectly compatible with regarding the good as "absolute," in so far as this term is used in some of its senses in popular speech (cf. PSL, p. 14). Thus the good may be said to be absolute in the sense of being fixed or constant to the extent that the organisms concerned and their environment remain constant. But the good cannot have a greater constancy or absoluteness than its ground; consequently, if we reject the dogmatic belief in the unalterable fixity of human nature or of the world, the notion of an absolutely and eternally fixed good goes with it. Secondly, the good may be said to be absolute, in that it rests upon a determinate and biologically rooted organization of impulses, as against being relative to some unauthoritative opinion. It is a predetermined irrational nature which finds distinctions between poison and food, happiness and misery, and not the opinion of some moralist except in so far as he may express this rooted natural basis. Finally, the good may be said to be absolute in the sense of being intrinsic and self-sufficient, rather than relative as means to some other good. The absoluteness of good will in such a case consist of its being ultimately final and all-sufficient, leaving nothing further to be desired. The ideal of the life of reason may be said to be absolute in this sense.

An immediate corollary of the doctrine that all value is relative to some desire is the fact that while there is a certain constancy or invariance of moral judgment in direct proportion to the constancy or uniformity of certain basic structures that characterize all human beings, there is also a natural diversity and plurality of individuals or groups constituted of different desires and attempting to satisfy different needs. Just as naturalism entails a rejection of the attempt to set up a realm of values apart from human interest and bias, values that would be pure and impartial, so again this principle tends to destroy the validity of all universal ethical judgments when used outside a specific context or frame of reference. Systems of right and wrong, good and bad, are as constant or as varied as cultures or bodies of interests happen to be.

Santayana recognizes elements both of flux and constancy, variability and invariance, in human nature. Only in so far as there are inherited, recurrent, and constant functions displaying themselves in all human beings, can a common morality be discovered; but to the extent that there are structural or functional differences among various cultures, classes, individuals, or groups, different moral standards in conformity with these differences are not only inevitable but justifiable (cf. LR, I, 280–81; "Two Rational Moralists," JPh, XIII [1916], 290 ff.). A certain rudimentary unanimity in preference and estimation among all human beings is founded on certain pervasive animal characteristics. "Mankind can never, without perishing, surrender its animal nature, its need to eat and drink, its sexual method of reproduction, its vision of nature, its faculty of speech, its arts of music, poetry, and building [LR, I, 287]." Diversities appear as we mark the differences that separate various social or cultural groups. While within such groups a certain moral integration or unanimity of thought and action may be latent or realized, nevertheless such unanimity does not extend beyond the limits of the respective needs and interests of these groups. Finally, there are significant individual differences which distinguish the specific character of every man from every other. If every individual

can know himself by expressing the entelechy of his own nature in the form of a consistent ideal, he is a rational creature after his own kind, even if, like the angels of Saint Thomas, he be the only individual of his species. What the majority of human animals may tend to, or what the past or future variations of a race may be, has nothing to do with determining the ideal of human nature in a living man, or in an ideal society of men bound together by spiritual kinship [LR, I, 280].

The life of reason as an ideal applies to each of these various levels of determinate behavior, from the characteristic activities of humanity at large down to the specific faculties and needs of different individuals.

A naturalistic approach to these matters, therefore, forces the recognition that in actual practice nature and human life are so organized that in certain respects a competition of interests and a clash of rival claims to self-preservation are inevitable. For existence is always finite, particular, and limited in time and place; hence the demands of different impulses, individuals, and groups are such that they are not all capable of realization. Whether we consider the competition of divergent impulses within the life of a single individual, or the differing interests of individuals within a group, or the innumerable moralities of groups themselves, the same situation prevails. Each interest, individual, or group is seeking to preserve its own existence against all enemies and to realize its own unique good over the goods of all others. Unanimity at any given time and place is a relative and limited matter; while a modification and discipline of interests may be effected, causing certain otherwise conflicting interests to move in unison, nevertheless some interests and faculties will always have to be sacrificed, will always remain outside the fold and alien to the imposed discipline.

Now from a naturalistic point of view, that is, from a point of view describing facts, rather than expressing a specific ideal or preference, disparate ideals are equally "good" and different perfectibilities are equally genuine. But they are good and genuine only from their own point of view, and not from the point of view of some other interest by which they might be judged. The existence of evil is the inevitable consequence of conflicting and irreconcilable interests struggling to preserve themselves in the same environment, the successful self-preservation of the victor involving the defeat of the victim. The success of the malaria germ represents the defeat of the person infected and, while we may pity the poor lamb devoured by the wolf, we must also remember the happy wolf. This natural or biological parity of ideals is a purely descriptive matter, not a moral one. It indicates that "moral distinctions are natural, that they arise and vary with the endeavours and interests of living beings [OS, p. 72]."

Such doctrine has immediate moral consequences (cf. OS, p. 69). First, while it recognizes a natural disparity of ideals, it is only aims sincerely held that are recognized as ideals. No shallow or merely verbal expression of interests may be reckoned as representing a competitor in the field of self-preservation. Ideals, to be recognized as aims of genuine impulses, must be deeply rooted and sincerely felt. Second, a recognition of the variability and natural legitimacy of different ideals demands chivalry in our attitude toward them.

I cannot help thinking [says Santayana] that a consciousness of the relativity of values, if it became prevalent, would tend to render people more truly social than would a belief that things have intrinsic and unchangeable values, no matter what the attitude of any one to them may be. If we said that goods, including the right distribution of goods, are relative to specific natures, moral warfare would continue, but not with poisoned arrows. Our private sense of justice itself would be acknowledged to have but a relative authority, and while we could not have a higher duty than to follow it, we should seek to meet those whose aims were incompatible with it as we meet things physically inconvenient, without insulting them as if they were morally vile or logically contemptible. Real unselfishness consists in sharing the interests of others. Beyond the pale of actual unanimity the only possible unselfishness is chivalry—a recognition of the inward right and justification of our enemies fighting against us [WD, p. 151].

The principle of naturalistic relativism or pluralism saves us from both the futility of moral absolutism and the blind belief that one's own ideal is the only good and one's own moral code the only embodiment of right conduct (cf. GTB, p. 27; EGP, pp. 167–68). The louder absolutisms proclaim the universal validity of their ideals and codes, the more clearly they betray the relative status of their judgments and the local and merely temporary origins of their preferences.

On an intellectual level, therefore, the principle of naturalism leads to a universal sympathy with all forms of perfection and all types of moralities. In widening the intellectual horizon, this principle lessens the possibility of fanaticism and increases the possibility of coöperation. On a practical level, however, the principle of naturalism confirms rather than weakens the necessity of some arbitrary principle in action.

We exist by distinction, by integration round a specific nucleus according to a particular pattern. Life demands a great insensibility as well as a great sensibility [GTB, pp. 7–8; cf. LR, IV, 109; RT, pp. 70–71].

There is thus a profound difference between a fanatical dogmatism that sets itself up as the absolute, sole expression of the ideal, and an inevitable arbitrariness that realizes its relativity and ultimate irrationality; it is the difference between moral absolutism and moral integrity. Education is capable of modifying our will and directing it along new channels to coöperate with other interests. But this is possible only when the structural capacities to adopt those interests are present. The ultimate appeal must be to some irrationally determined need or desire. "Unanimity in thought involves identity of functions and similarity in organs. These conditions mark off the sphere of rational communication and society; where they fail altogether there is no mutual intelligence, no conversation, no moral solidarity [LR, I, 278; cf. LR, V, 247, 256–61; WD. pp. 148 ff.; LR, I, 152–53]."

A recognition of the facts about human life which we have just briefly summarized as constituting a naturalistic approach —namely, facts as to the continuity of human nature and nature as a whole, the givenness of the determinate structure of human faculties and habits, and of the laws governing material events, the ground of value or ideality in interest or impulse, and the natural variety in the animal and human world of such interests and their corresponding values—is necessary, though not sufficient, for an understanding of the structure of the life of reason. That moral theories, such as those of Christianity and some forms of Platonism, did not represent these conditions adequately is a prime reason for their ultimate failure. For "to misrepresent the conditions and consequences of action is no merely speculative error; it involves a false emphasis in character and an artificial balance and co-ordination among human pursuits[LR, I, 11]."

Nevertheless, while natural science in general "may furnish a theatre and properties for our drama," it "offers no hint of its plot and meaning." For example, the fact that the grounds of preference in conduct are immediate desires, leaves undetermined the question of the desirability of various actions. Were naturalism in this respect the only principle of ethics, moral anarchy and pure barbarism would be the sole realities, since the only test or standard of conduct would be identical with the actual expression, however irrational, of uncontrolled desire and unreflective impulse. Again, to be aware of the given materials of human conduct or natural mechanism does not tell us what might be accomplished with the given. And finally, the recognition of competing interests is the awareness of a problematic situation, not a solution of it. Since divergent claims of opposing interests cannot be realized immediately within a finite existence, some regimen or moral order is demanded. If habits did not conflict with new interests and if each impulse as it arose could be satisfied in turn without preventing the satisfaction of another interest, there would be no moral problem at all. Intelligence is necessary when conflict arises, and this means, not that the irrational core of impulses and needs be subverted altogether, but, on the contrary, that this core become conscious of its ends and that it proceed to satisfy its demands in the most harmonious manner. The conflict between impulses within the life of a single individual, the conflict between the competing needs of the individuals in a given group, and the conflict between societies themselves, together with their different moral and political interests, set the stage and pose the problem.

What is genuinely desirable, what is to be achieved by the use of the given, what means are to be employed in effecting a possible harmony of conflicting impulses, all these are questions that intelligence, confronted with these facts about human nature, must solve, if a genuine ideality is to supervene.

Intelligence.—The principle of naturalism, as we have seen, emphasizes, among other things, the necessary connection between value and desire; it denies the validity of the attempt to set up a realm of transcendent values apart from human enjoyment, selection, or preference. All values must be rooted in actual need. In itself, however, this principle is insufficient for a moral theory of the rational life since to assert such a connection would be to neglect an equally important consideration, namely, that such values require the certification of critical judgment and intelligent analysis if they are to be admitted to the rational life. Values set up independent of intelligence are as inadmissible as values regarded as independent of all desire. Genuine values are neither purely immediate satisfactions of irrational impulse nor superempirical rational objects of purely intellectual understanding. They are, in the rational life, participants of both irrationality and intelligence, being rooted in animal desire and immediate pleasures on the one hand and intelligently pursued or embodied on the other. The good is thus neither objectively independent of all interest nor identical with whatever is desired or felt. The good is the desirable, that which can be progressively and harmoniously enacted as the result of intelligent action.

The principle of naturalism acquaints us with the *causes* of our preferences and dislikes. It describes the natural basis and origins of all ideals. The principle of intelligent criticism, on the other hand, demands, in addition, *reasons* in the form of carefully analyzed and deliberated judgments for those same preferences or dislikes. The office of intelligence is the articulation of desires and intent, with a view to selecting those specific modes of satisfaction which contribute to a fuller, more enduring happiness. Intelligent criticism, in short, is a name for that method in conduct which, by revealing the interconnections of that conduct, enables irrational and immediate bias or interest to express itself in rational, responsible, and perfected ways, rather than blindly and without foresight or genuine freedom.

This modification of action by intelligence is, however, only a matter of degree, since even in the most elementary moral experiences of value there is, in addition to the purely emotional and immediate satisfaction of some impulse, a germ of deliberate judgment and critical understanding of the ideal aimed at. This is true, for example, of what Santayana calls pre-rational morality, or that which is

non-dialectical, casual, impulsive, polyglot. . . . There is indeed reason in it, since every deliberate precept expresses some reflection by which impulses have been compared and modified. But such chance reflection amounts to moral perception, not to moral science. . . . On this stage, in the moral world, are the judgments of Mrs. Grundy, the aims of political parties and their maxims, the principles of war, the appreciation of art, the commandments of religious authorities, special revelations of duty to individuals, and all systems of intuitive ethics [LR, V, 211–12; cf. LR, IV, 192].

The application of intelligence is simply the renewed concentration upon the element of criticism in order to enlarge the scope of conscious ideals, more adequately to conceive their inner structure and external relations, and thereby to insure their practical harmony with other interests similarly analyzed. Reason in the sphere of obligation is but conscience deepened, and rational ethics but habitual or impulsive conduct enlightened and made aware of its partialities and failures. The difference that intelligence makes is the difference between a morality that is nearsighted, inconsistent, and lacking in scope, and one distinguished by the opposite of these qualities. The difference between impulsive and genuine ideals, between apparent and real goods, like the difference between faith in unverified beliefs and experimentally validated hypotheses in science, or like the difference between mere taste and critical judgment in art, is a difference that method makes. In one case there is merely a stubborn and blind assertion of desire, faith, or taste; in the other these immediate reactions are submitted to a process of inquiry by which these claims must acquire an eventual validation if they are to survive. Ideals, beliefs, and tastes, directed upon goodness, truth, and beauty, have to justify themselves and must establish their claim to reveal or to embody these qualities. And this revelation or embodiment is not something given; it has to be won by labor, by intelligence, by piecemeal analysis. The fall of Adam from a state of divine perfection, where goodness, truth, and beauty are facts at hand in Paradise, to be immediately enjoyed, to a state where he has to work by the sweat of his brow to regain these, is an ancient symbol for this human situation. The principle of critical intelligence is the necessary reminder of the fact that there are no short cuts to Paradise.

In this respect the emphasis upon intelligence as the method for distinguishing apparent from real goods, impulsive from genuine ideals, comes to supplant the mythical criterion provided by an overrigorous and unnaturalistic Platonism in religion and philosophy. In these a sharp distinction is set up between "eternal values," or those which the will of God assures and sanctions, and the "current valuations of the worldling," or those which are wholly momentary, fugitive, and illusory. The distinction is then made to hang upon some system of supernatural forces, producing and sustaining some values, while denying or neglecting others. Though some distinction should be made between the desired and the desirable, since otherwise there would be no meaning to the moral enterprise, nevertheless it is a distinction which reason and experience must make, and not some alien and imposed system of arbitrary rules.

Intelligence is the practical side of reason. One implication of the title of the book, *The Life of Reason,* is that an understanding of the nature of reason is to be had by examining its rôle in the specific contexts of the various types of experience that constitute life. The attempt to isolate reason and to study its properties and functions apart from this context is designated by Santayana "visionary insolence." The only valid procedure is to study reason in act, reason as it operates in individual behavior, in society, religion, art, and science. When so studied it is seen to be primarily practical. That is to say, it is a method applied and devoted to the perfection of interests whose initial expressions are crude and irrational.

Reason as method is prescriptive only with reference to the form or order that its objects are to possess. It makes no demands on the materials or elements which shall enter into an aspired or actual harmony. "The materials for the synthesis are such at each point as nature and accident have made them[GTB, pp. 61–62]." Materials are presented in the form of specific problems and entertained ideals as these are expressed by any interest—artistic, social, religious, or scientific. In taking the point of view of these interests, the end of intelligence is nothing other than their perfection, their harmony with one another: "every art and every activity involves a congruous good, and . . . the endeavor to realize the ideal in every direction is an effort of which reason necessarily approves, since reason is nothing but the method of that endeavor[LR, V, 265; cf. LR, IV, 109]." Its work is accomplished when adequate poems, theories, states, prayers, and the objects of innumerable other interests are brought into being. To call any of these a "rational" product is simply to call attention to the method of its production.

What, then, is the general method of intelligence as it intervenes between a given irrational datum and the finished ideal product that it helps to create? Santayana's answer is that it consists of attention to two primary facts. It develops the ideal import and the significant relations of a given purpose and it insures the relevance of that elaborated purpose to actual matters of fact. Clarity of purpose and docility to fact —to know one's mind and to accommodate that mind to the given facts—these are the prerequisites of intelligent conduct.

Intelligence consists in having read the heart and deciphered the promptings latent there, and then in reading the world and deciphering its law and constitution, to see how and where the heart's ideal may be embodied. . . . We fail in practical affairs when we ignore the conditions of action and we fail in works of imagination when we concoct what is fantastic and without roots in the world[LR, IV, 222].

Intelligence is at once a faculty of idealization and a means of checking this idealization by keeping it relevant and applicable to what can actually be performed. It thus serves to connect the other two principles of the life of reason, naturalism and moral idealism, the emphasis respectively upon given facts and genuine ideals:

The paths of life are many, and most of them without issue. Knowledge of nature and of self, in clarifying the blind materialism of action, enlightens this choice of direction, proves it to have been fruitful, and enables it still to be so. The steady habit of matter within, in the psyche, meets and feeds on its steady variations without; and life attains the dignity of the rational animal. Without this definition in character and this recognition of matter, life can only grope and flounder, vehemently agitated by a vague wretchedness, without either courage to confess its limits or lucidity to see its goal [RM, p. 202].

The power of intellectual synthesis, or what Santayana also calls the dialectic analysis of intent, is the mental counterpart of the overt power of acting in accordance with the changing and ordered facts of the external world. Both are integral, necessary, and continuous aspects of a single method. The first is the preliminary rehearsal, comparison, and analysis on a discursive level of the inner structure and relations of an ideal, whereas the second is the experimental manipulation and material realization of those ideals selected and represented by prior critical inquiry. As such, these two phases of method when applied to conduct are illustrations of scientific method in general, the cardinal traits of which are a logical exploration and systematic organization of possible hypotheses, and confirmation of these hypotheses and their implications in terms of observed matters of fact.

Socrates, the first to realize this function of intelligence in ethical matters, emphasized the first of these factors and demanded that

rationality, in the form of an examination and clarification of purposes, should precede any selection of external instruments. For how should a man recognize anything useful unless he first had established the end to be subserved and thereby recognized the good? [LR, V, 243].

From the moderns, including Spencer, Darwin, and the pragmatists, Santayana derives his emphasis on the second of these factors, the necessary docility and adjustment to external facts.

Man exists amid a universal ferment of being, and not only needs plasticity in his habits and pursuits but finds plasticity also in the surrounding world. Life is an equilibrium which is maintained now by accepting modification and now by imposing it [LR, IV, 3].

The dialectic analysis of intent means the clarification of purposes by discursively analyzing their essential structure and possible relations to other interests. It is simply using the Socratic method of inquiry to discover what we really want, as contrasted with what we seem to want on the spur of the moment and at the bidding of some immediate impulse. Without articulate and fixed purposes, without ideals consciously entertained, action collapses into mere motion and activity into mere change. Habit or impulse, examples of activity without consciousness of relations or foresight of consequences, are, as often as not, frustrated by unforeseen external circumstances or by the pressure of other interests. When intelligence is applied to habit or impulse, the demands of the latter are analyzed in the light of the represented demands of other interests, as well as in the light of the available forces of the material environment necessary to their realization. Thus the immediate demands of hunger become transformed into a conscious ideal, first, when a perfect understanding is had of the nutritive value of various foods; furthermore when the connection between food and flour, seeds, and cultivation of land is perceived; and finally, when the demand for food is harmonized with other relevant demands, such as those for pleasant taste or congenial surroundings while eating. The principle that this trivial example illustrates is applicable throughout the sphere of the rational life.

Conscious ideals, the directive purposes of intelligent action, differ on the one hand from mere impulse or craving, and on the other from merely entertained, speculative ideals. In distinction from the latter there is present a necessary impulsive drive, an irrational, sincere, and prompting need agitating for its satisfaction. One condition that an ideal must fulfill is that

it must be a resultant or synthesis of impulses already afoot. An ideal out of relation to the actual demands of living beings is so far from being an ideal that it is not even a good [LR, I, 260].

In distinction from mere impulse, moreover, there is present in the conscious ideal the necessary intellectual factor, the consciousness of relations to other demands, and an understanding of the means for realizing its own perfection.

Man's rational life consists in those moments in which reflection not only occurs but proves efficacious. What is absent then works in the present, and values are imputed where they cannot be felt. Such representation is so far from being merely speculative that its presence alone can raise bodily change to the dignity of action. Reflection gathers experiences together and perceives their relative worth; which is as much as to say that it expresses a new attitude of will in the presence of a world better understood and turned to some purpose [LR, I, 2–3].

Santayana gives a simple illustration of this function of intelligence in tracing dialectically the relations and consequences of any imagined ideal, in order to determine its possible harmony with other interests.

A vessel's true excellence is more deeply conditioned than the shipwright may imagine when he prides himself on having made something that will float and go. The best battle-ship, or racing yacht, or freight steamer, might turn out to be a worse thing for its specific excellence, if the action it facilitated proved on the whole maleficent, and if war or racing or trade could be rightly condemned by a philosopher. The rationality of ship-building has several sets of conditions; the patron's demands must first be fulfilled: then the patron's specifications have to be judged by the purpose he in turn has in mind; this purpose itself has to be justified by his ideal in life, and finally, his ideal by its adequacy to his total ultimate nature. Error on any of these planes makes the ultimate product irrational [LR, IV, 18].

The second factor that serves to define intelligence is the ability to learn from experience—docility and adjustment to necessary facts. The moral validity of conceived ideals is determined by their efficacy in practice, their verification in actual conduct. While it is possible to treat ideals as objects of pure contemplation without taking any steps toward enacting them, nevertheless intelligence and the impulse that prompted that contemplation would be cheated in those circumstances, and what should, properly regarded, be an instrument of art is truncated at a stage before the art is made possible. Hell is paved with good intentions but a successful life requires action.

Reason is only half grown and not really distinguishable from imagination so long as she cannot check and recast her own processes wherever they render the moulds of thought unfit for their subject-matter. Docility . . . is the deepest condition of reason's existence [LR, I, 202; cf. LR, IV, 12; GTB, p. 59].

The intent working in thought or in will has a transitive or transcendent function; it regards things external to it. This is a necessary condition of an animal whose body is in constant external relations with its environment. The function of intelligence in this situation is therefore not merely one of consistency or unity of purpose, but also of correspondence with relevant facts—the past, present, and future, the near and the far. The effectiveness of this correspondence or adjustment is a measure of man's ability to learn from and to anticipate experience.

Docility or plasticity in habits is exercised in a twofold direction—upon the mutual adjustment of various interests of conduct, and upon the relation of those interests to the material environment. Docility in the first direction takes the form of sacrifice and discipline of the impulses, in the second of practical adjustment to external forces. When applied to the stuff of conduct, the multiplicity of impulses, intelligence enforces the need for renouncing certain demands only so that others may be more effectively realized in the end. "Sacrifice first becomes possible, and constantly necessary, in a way-ward being imperfectly unified; and in him it may be fruitful, because by restraining each of his impulses on occasion, and discharging them only in a certain measure and in a certain order, a decent harmony can be established among them [OS, pp. 271–72; cf. LR, I, 258 ff.]. When used in reference to the relation of impulses and the natural environment, intelligence becomes the method that seeks for the mutual adjustment and harmonious interaction of these factors. On the plane of knowledge this docility appears in the verified truth of ideas; on the plane of material action, in the proper balancing of material forces.

The foregoing is a brief summary of Santayana's conception of the *ideal* function of intelligence in the rational life. If, however, we consider the historic process wherein some form of ideality is approached or achieved, intelligence represents but one among the many forces that operate. The development from natural conditions to ideal goals is not always deliberately conscious nor intelligently purposeful. Santayana is careful to avoid the exploded rationalisms of some eighteenth-century philosophies that would endow all change with inherent rationality and conscious forethought, such as is involved, for example, in attributing the development of language or of various religious and social institutions to some carefully thought-out plan. It is a lesson driven home by the nineteenth century and by the biological emphasis of pragmatism that intelligence is at most a casual, though important instrument of adjustment in a largely irrational train of events.

One function of intelligence is the recognition of the reason for this situation. Intelligence knows that it alone is by no means sufficient in a world that contains so many hampering

irrationalities. It knows that men are often unfaithful to
their own ideals and that the outcome of much action is con-
siderably removed from original aspirations. Yet in recognizing its own frailty as well as the irreducible element of
contingency in the world and in experience, it insists that
the part of wisdom is to accept what is inevitable, in order
to change what is not. The life of reason as an ideal is defined;
its progressive realization consists in overcoming surmount-
able difficulties, in order to achieve the maximum rationality
possible within given limits. But "the inner authority of reason . . . is no more destroyed because it has limits in physical expression or because irrational things exist, than the
grammar of a given language is invalidated because other
languages do not share it, or because some people break its
rules and others are dumb altogether [LR, I, 278-79]."

The ideal.—The fruit of experience, that which justifies
human existence and intelligent action, is moral idealism, the
conception and embodiment of ideal perfections. The groundwork existing in natural faculties, habits, and impulses, and
the critical work of intelligence in clearing the waste and providing some order in this material, issue, in the rational life,
in the imaginative intuition of life's ultimate values and in the
artful transition to their embodiment.

The environing world can justify itself to the mind only by the free
life which it fosters there. All observation is observation of brute
fact, all discipline is mere repression, until these facts digested and
this discipline embodied in humane impulses become the starting-
point for a creative movement of the imagination, the firm basis for
ideal constructions in society, religion, and art. Only as conditions
of these human activities can the facts of nature and history become
morally intelligible or practically important. In themselves they are
trivial incidents, gossip of the Fates, cacklings of their inexhaustible
garrulity. To regard the function of man as accomplished when these
chance happenings have been recorded by him or contributed to by
his impulsive action, is to ignore his reason, his privilege,—shared
for the rest with every living creature,—of using Nature as food and

substance for his own life. This human life is not merely animal and passionate. The best and keenest part of it consists in that very gift of creation and government which, together with all the transcendental functions of his own mind, man has significantly attributed to God as to his highest ideal. Not to see in this rational activity the purpose and standard of all life is to have left human nature half unread[PR, pp. viii–ix; cf. SB, p. 262; WD, p. 183].

The term "moral idealism" with Santayana has a double meaning, signifying at once the definition of ideals imaginatively entertained and the fact of enjoyed perfections actually realized in some material. An ideal may mean either the *object* of some desire or the *terminus* of some activity. To the thirsty traveler water is the *ideal object* of his impulse. The elimination of his thirst when he drinks the water is the ideal *end* or completion of his quest. A moral ideal in the first case is the representation or symbolic rendering of some desired perfection; in the second it is a name for the perfect experience actually undergone and lived through. Moral idealism is used as a name for the principle of selection, aspiration, and protest in experience, the imaginative devotion to and definition of ideals; and as a name for the ideals embodied by art, where the latter term may be used in its widest signification as synonymous with the life of reason. The first meaning points to a force working within experience, the principle of direction and aspiration; the second points to ideals achieved, to finished products, to ends achieved by art. In the latter case, "like art, . . . the Life of Reason is not a power but a result, the spontaneous expression of liberal genius in a favouring environment[LR, I, 6]." In human life, therefore, if not in the world at large, moral idealism is all-important, since it constitutes a teleological principle of explanation, a justifying goal of conduct, and an intrinsic standard of excellence. It rescues life from futility, it provides something to live for.

Since life is essentially a form of natural transition or a

process, and not a congealed, timeless reality, it involves at all points elements of incompleteness, anticipation, and uncertainty of outcome. In conscious life, and especially in a life guided by intelligence, imagined prospects or ends-in-view become ideals to guide action, promises of perfect fulfillment of function. This situation is one of which, given this fact of natural transition, reason itself approves. For idealism, in the sense of a conscious, critical representation of goods of action, is a necessary prerequisite of action that is to be free—that is, enlightened about the probable outcome of its career, and voluntary—that is, possessed of the power of choosing among possible alternative ends.

Moral idealism as a principle of selection, protest, and aspiration in experience is defined on the one hand by an enlightened intent upon determinate forms, a guidance of art in the reformation of the actual; and on the other, by a correlative protest against the already existent, in so far as the latter contains imperfections, error, and confusion. An idealist is one who is at once devoted to what ought to be, passionately aware of some definite good, and condemnatory of the actual for its shortcomings and evils.

In a rational life, however, the conception of moral idealism involves the rejection of three extremes, namely, romanticism, pantheism, and Platonism of the magical variety.

Romanticism, or the miscellaneous, random, and uncontrolled pursuit of any and all ideals, must be avoided. Rather one must define specific and determinate goals, and not put all one's energies into pursuing infinite and limitless forms of perfection, nor exhaust oneself in the attempt to find the ultimate value of life in mere pursuit, experience, or "life." Santayana, as a representative of the classic traditions of Greek and Catholic civilization, emphasizes the need for form and discipline in experience. He rejects the immaturity and romantic willfulness of German moralists, who regard the mere removal of restraints and the absence of determinate form as itself an indication of the achievement of some good. While, indeed, no empirically given form may be of such a character that it provides an eternally stable organization or adjustment of necessary forces (thus causing revolution and arousing neglected interests to press for their satisfaction in some more just economy), nevertheless the alternative to this state of affairs is not that of abandoning form altogether but rather that of instituting some more representative and stable equilibrium.

The romantic ideal is, properly speaking, no ideal at all. In putting all its emphasis on the variety, immediacy, and apparent groundlessness of experience as it is presented in action, memory, or soliloquy, it renounces any fixed, single goal that might serve as an ideal of achievement. The romantic is incapable of learning anything through his endless exploits. Romanticism is rich and exciting; it is not chastened and informed. The romantic is fundamentally a barbarian or a child, for whom the will opens up an infinite vista of possible interests, but who remains undisciplined as he passes from one to the other without any ordered sequence, wisdom, or rational choice. He lacks two things: a knowledge of the natural limits and conditions of things, and a clear consciousness of the specific goals or ideals of conduct selected by self-knowledge and through experience (cf. TPP, pp. 139 ff.; EGP, pp. 116 ff.). The moral idealism of the rational life, however, is directed precisely upon these two facts. The ideals proper to an individual or to a group are only such as their limited and endowed nature makes possible. The ends an individual will seek will be those which he is capable of attaining. "In morals the infinite is a chimera, and . . . in accomplishing anything definite a man renounces everything else [LR, II, 35; cf. SB, pp. 127–28, 147; LR, I, 261]." Moral idealism is a principle of *selection*, and the necessary complement of selection is renunciation. That the devotion of energies to chosen interests involves the sacrifice of others is the moral analogue of the metaphysical axiom that all determination involves negation.

Secondly, moral idealism in a rational life involves a rejection of pantheism, or the belief that whatever exists is right or good. For pantheism from an ethical point of view is the result of identifying the ideal with the actual, since the notion of God is simply that of a perfect being. (When God is interpreted as constituting the realm of essence, the neutral and infinite realm of all possible forms, pantheism is equally objectionable in Santayana's view, this time on metaphysical grounds, for pantheism then asserts the natural embodiment in the realm of matter of the entire realm of essence.) Pantheism, to the extent that it involves an identification of the actual and the ideal, becomes an apology for all existing evils, a denial of moral idealism. This position, common to the systems of the Stoics, Hegel, and Royce, teaches that all evil, whether in the past, the present, or the future, is simply an indispensable part of the total goodness of the universe. Evils are apparent deficiencies merely from our limited, partial points of view. Really and from the point of view of the whole, they conspire to form an ideal structure. But this system, which commonly goes by the name of idealism, is in fact a contempt for all ideals, slavishly accepting whatever happens to exist as already ideal; as such "it appeals mightily to the powers that be, in Church and in State[WD, p. 162]."

In contrast to this doctrine, the moral idealism of the life of reason is a frank recognition of the relativity of all goods and evils to experiencing subjects. There is no single, absolute point of view from which one can say that everything is good (or evil); there are only finite, pluralistic systems of values, finding real satisfactions or frustrations as the case may be. If we were pure spirits, we should have a sympathetic

love for every good pursued, since we should have none of
our own with which these others might possibly conflict; but
we are not pure spirits, so that while

reason may be the *differentia* of man, it is surely not his essence. His
essence, at best, is animality qualified by reason [OS, p. 290].

The part of moral idealism for man, therefore, is "to distinguish, in this bad or mixed reality, the part, however small,
that could be loved and chosen from the remainder, however
large, which was to be rejected and renounced [BHMO,
pp. 246–47; cf. LR, III, 140 ff., 164; OS, pp. 82, 85 ff.]."
Moral idealism as it functions in the rational life is a principle of *protest* against real and existent evils, a preliminary
step in the reformation of the actual.

Finally, moral idealism involves a rejection of Platonism,
where this means turning the ideal into a superempirical
power or force serving as a magnet for action, a material influence for the course of events. The ideal does not exist in
some heaven from which it directs the course of events below;
it is simply the possible form of some material fact, brought
into being by the efficacy of material instruments. In Platonism, however, the hypostasis of ideas constitutes a super-
numerary world or second physics, a world existing outside of
the natural cosmos and somehow regulating it. The beings
composing this realm are fixed and distinct models of goods,
existing independently of all valuation by any finite being,
yet at the same time exercising a miraculous control over
formless matter and inducing it to imitate their forms. Aside
from the superstitious and entirely mythical physics involved,
this theory forfeits its entire right to be regarded as the
expression of a genuine moral idealism, for it cuts itself off
from all earthly attachment and moral striving. When an
ideal is converted into a substance, "it is only a ghostly existence, with no more moral significance or authority in relation
to the observer than has any happy creature which may hap-

pen to exist somewhere in the unknown reaches of the universe [LR, III, 135; cf. PSL, p. 3]."

Ideals, rather, define the possible excellences of things and conduct, goals which human beings aspire to reach. Good men, bridles, or governments, are those that realize perfectly their specific functions. These functions are not controlled magically from above, but discover their adequate form in experience and use. Furthermore, if an imagined ideal is to become effectively embodied, some transition to it must be possible from the existing state of affairs. The development from the natural to the ideal must be possible of fulfillment. Moral idealism in the rational life is at all points necessarily allied to the natural basis of that life; it embraces no ideals but those that foreshadow some improvement upon the already existent, that come to satisfy some need felt, and to the realization of which some bridging mechanism can be found. "Ideals would be irrelevant if they were not natural entelechies, if they were not called for by something that exists and if, consequently, their realization would not be a present and actual good [TCWJ, II, 320–21; cf. LR, III, 248–49]." Moral idealism is a principle of *aspiration,* not a doctrine of antecedently existing causal agencies.

When we consider moral life as a process of growth from natural to ideal conditions, moral idealism may be taken as a name for those factors which constitute the perfections or intrinsic idealities possible to various activities, impulses, and institutions. An ideal, in the sense of an embodied perfection, is the end of which an ideal in the sense of a representation of that perfection is the means. For the life of reason, ideals as imaginatively anticipated perfections occupy an intermediate stage in a career the proper end of which is the embodiment of those ideals, the morally last stage of the process. In this sense, therefore, the relative perfections of rational religion, moral science, and art, in achieving some vision or representation of life's ideals, are preliminary rehearsals in symbols of what, for an enacted rational life, would constitute enjoyed realities.

The excellence of religion [for example] is due to an idealization of experience which, while making religion noble if treated as poetry, makes it necessarily false if treated as science. Its function is rather to draw from reality materials for an image of that ideal to which reality ought to conform, and to make us citizens, by anticipation, in the world we crave [PR, p. vi].

In the architectonic of a life of reason, such symbols serve as representations of what life for society and the individual might be. Just as there is a distinction between an imagined goal of unenlightened impulse and the actual satisfaction of such impulse (which may not be at all *satisfactory,* precisely because it is immediate and unrelated to other impulses), so, too, there is a distinction between the representation of a genuine ideal and its embodiment or realization in action. The one is wholly symbolic and imaginative; the other possesses the dimension of living content, the harmonies the organization of which are summed up in consciousness and accompanied by the awareness of the exact finalities achieved.

A doctrine of intrinsic or final goods defines the genuine and ultimate ends of conduct without which all effort and experience would not be rationally justifiable. It saves us from the futilities of romanticism and philistinism. The former illustrates a continual state of flux without any specific direction, and the latter a continual state of servility to means, or exaggerated respect for instrumentalities, without any consciousness of the ends these might properly serve (cf. LR, III, 200 ff.).

The distinction between instrumental and final goods is in no way, of course, incompatible with the principle of naturalistic relativism or the insistence that all goods are relative to the interest of some individual or group. The relativity of goods to desire does not remove the distinction that is necessary between goods valuable as means and goods that are self-justifying and final. An ideal is an end, therefore, in both senses of this term; it is the finally perfect form achieved in a process of development, an end with respect to the career of its varied appearances, and it is an end with respect to the materials and activities that serve as means for its realization.

Felt needs and desires constitute the natural basis of any genuine ideal. It is precisely because the ideal itself is rooted in desire that it can confront with its own achievement other modes of expression of the same irrational forces, thereby making evident their shortcomings. Before the ideal super-venes, each impulse seeks its own good, independent of the demands or wishes of all others. Its blindness and haste, however, soon lead it to ruin, for there are inevitable enemies and material forces in the form of other impulses that are equally insistent upon their own satisfaction. In the face of such defeat, reflection may suggest some means for attain-ing success. For the ideal that a circumspect intelligence helps to establish is now composed of all compatible interests, so organized and transformed that instead of being irrecon-cilably antagonistic to one another, they contribute to a rep-resentative and mutually supporting harmony. Yet unless the ideal were based on and included these interests or impulses, however modified and domesticated they may now be, it could have no moral force and constitute no genuine improve-ment. "An ideal representing no living interest would be irrelevant to practice, just as a conception of reality would be irrelevant to perception which should not be composed of the materials that sense supplies, or should not re-embody actual sensations in an intelligible system [LR, I, 259–60]."

It is this retention by the ideal of a natural basis in living demands that distinguishes the life of reason from mysticism, asceticism, and spirituality of an otherworldly sort. For in each of these cases the attempt is made to pass beyond good and evil by subverting the natural basis of all desire. Yet such an escape is impossible of complete fulfillment, for if life even on its lowest vegetative level is not to cease altogether, some discrimination, feeling, and preference must remain. The good is to be sought by incorporating relevant natural demands and needs, rather than by attempting to repress them altogether.

It is not sufficient, however, that the ideal have this natural basis in extant demands; its form must be such that these demands can coexist harmoniously and mutually support one another. The discipline and sacrifice imposed on the parts, so that the whole may acquire the desirable form, renders the will consistent—since there will be no contrary movements pulling in opposite directions, and harmonious—since each element will contribute its own perfection to the whole. This conception of harmony is organic in the sense that the constituent elements of every ideal must themselves be ideal.

If we consider science, for example, as a single activity possessing as its general ideal the discovery of truth, then each subdivision of science in turn must achieve its specific ideal (e. g., the discovery of truth about historical matters, about the physical constitution of the universe, about the psychological nature of human behavior, about the principles of logic and mathematics, or about the ethical purposes of conduct) if the general ideal is itself to be attained. Or again, the ideal family illustrates a coöperation of interests among its members:

The husband has an interest in protecting the wife, she in serving the husband. The weaker gains in authority and safety, the wilder and more unconcerned finds a help-mate at home to take thought for his daily necessities. Parents lend their children experience and a vicarious memory; children endow their parents with a vicarious immortality [LR, II, 36].

Or, to take a final example, health is the perfection of bodily functions, each of which performs its activity adequately and in unison with the others.

In general, then, "measure is a condition of perfection, for perfection requires that order should be pervasive, that not only the whole before us should have a form, but that every part in turn should have a form of its own, and that those parts should be coördinated among themselves as the whole is coördinated with the other parts of some greater cosmos [PR, p. 252]." The latter part of this statement calls attention to the fact that what in any given case is taken to constitute the substance of the ideal, as compared with the ideal itself, is a relative matter. The resultant organic unity of any particular ideal may function as a part of some wider, more inclusive, and representative ideal. In this sense, for example, from the point of view of the life of reason as a cultural ideal, science represents but one phase of a wider complex, in which its own ideal (however complicated in turn that might be) must be adjusted in an interfunctional harmony with the ideals of religion and art. Likewise, bodily health is but one aspect of the total ideal of a complete personality, just as the family is but one form of a natural society possessing the wider dimensions of economic and governmental activity.

What in any given case will constitute the relative order of inclusion and subordination of ideal materials depends on a hierarchy of values. It is the privilege of every living creature to set up his own scale of values and to assert his own preferences. This scale for him has but two necessary conditions, first that his preferences be grounded in his given faculties, habits, and interests, since no ideal or scheme of values can have any appeal to a man who has not the power or natural faculty to adopt that scheme; and second, that the particular gradation or order of preference be determined by an intelligent clarification of which ideals will stand higher after analysis of their representative scope and inclusiveness. The greater the rational value of an ideal is, the greater its representative power:

> The various ideals and types of perfection themselves, if a vital interest finds them propitious or antipathetic, are qualified and graded morally in view of that interest; and they could not otherwise be judged at all. Truly . . . among various perfections one is as perfect as another, and a perfect glove is as truly perfect as a perfect family: but I, being a naturalist, do not feel compelled to assert in consequence that a perfect family is not the greater good. Perfections may be differently prized, though each be as perfect as every other, because various sorts of perfect objects are not of equal consequence to a given animal nor in a given ideal. . . . Just because goods are relative to living interests, each interest may establish a hierarchy among the several goods it recognizes, according to the depth and force of its need for them. Various kinds of good are incommensurable only when the living interests that posit them are wholly disparate. Thus, it might be impossible to compare the intrinsic value of a perfect gnat with that of a perfect elephant or the intrinsic value of mere love with that of mere knowledge; yet the gnat and the elephant, love and knowledge might perfectly well have comparable and unequal values for the interests and in the environment of a third party [OS, pp. 72–73; cf. SB, p. 128].

An essential corollary of the naturalism of the moral theory of the life of reason is the legitimate variability and plurality of different scales of values. Not only is there no single nor absolute system for all individuals, but this very plurality is further increased by the fact that any individual might conceivably change his scheme of values within his own lifetime, in accordance with changing personal or environmental circumstances (cf. RT. p. 75). Since preferences are thus a function of specific natures and variable conditions, the whole concept of a scheme of heirarchy of values is one that relates to specific situations and specific preferences. A scheme of values is fixed or constant only in proportion to the constancy of the materials involved, namely, interests and environment; it varies with them and cannot be more stable than they.

Harmony is the structure of the rational life, sustained happiness its quality, the former being the condition for the latter. Santayana differs from the utilitarians and agrees with Aristotle in the belief that pleasure is not the direct aim of conduct but its by-product, the sign of perfected activity. Pleasure does not constitute a principle of direction, it does not indicate the necessary conditions for or method of attainment of some harmonious adjustment (cf. LR, V, 256–57). These principles and conditions are provided, rather, by natural disposition or capacity and by critical intelligence; pleasure and happiness arise when these have been successfully realized in action. A distinction, moreover, may be made between pleasure and happiness, not so much in terms of their differences in quality as in terms of their scope. For pleasure is the result of satisfied impulse, isolated, specific, and unconnected with the aims or satisfactions of other interests. Happiness, on the other hand, is to the rational harmony of an integrated will as pleasure is to the random, uncontrolled, and pre-rational interests of an undisciplined will. The distinction, in short, is between transient gratification and enduring, stable, reinforcing conduct. In either case the qualities of behavior denoted by the terms "pleasant" or "happy," cannot be divorced from the activities they adjectivally describe. If happiness be conceived as the highest good, it must not be conceived as the special good of a specific interest. Happiness is the sum and residual quality of all the multiple, variable goods upon which a given life is directed. It is not a final stage reached, a moment enjoyed at the end of a temporal process or during it; it is the form of the process of rational living itself.

THE SPIRITUAL LIFE

Two interpretations of "the spiritual life."—The foregoing exposition of the structure of the life of reason has been intended to convey what I take to be the essential moral philosophy of Santayana, the fitting complement to his general realistic methodology and naturalistic metaphysics. Santayana himself by temperament has always evidenced a preference for Olympian detachment and the rôle of the spectator. And that his philosophy should ultimately have emerged, in his later writings, with an emphasis upon the contemplative life is perfectly intelligible in the light of this interest. It reminds one of the way in which Spinoza climaxed his *Ethics* with the doctrine of the intellectual love of God, and of Aristotle's praises of the contemplative life in Book X of the *Nicomechean Ethics*.

The subject matter of *The Life of Reason* is the setting of intelligence and imagination in the context of practical adjustment to a material world, the organization of personal and social impulses into a life of harmony. The power of knowledge as an instrument for transforming natural and human situations receives greater attention than the ability of reason and imagination themselves to fascinate the mind by the spectacle they present. The freedom described in *The Life of Reason,* accordingly, is a freedom from bondage, barbarism, and disease; whereas the freedom of the spiritual life, the description of which forms the subject matter of the later writings, is that of an abstracted and sublimated detachment of the intellect devoted to vision for its own sake. Just as impulse contributes the *raison d'être* of moral idealism in the life of reason, so the detachment of the spiritual life determines its emphasis upon idealism in the altogether different sense of "thought and love fixed upon essence[RM, p. 190]."

The moment we ask, however, what, exactly, this detachment involves, what is to be understood by "thought and love fixed upon essence," we are confronted by a situation that bears some similarity to that which we encountered when we considered Santayana's general metaphysical position. For there are at least two ways in which we may construe the spiritual life: one makes it a legitimate vocation within a widely conceived life of reason, the other a form of postrational morality radically inconsistent with the general principles of rational ethics. This is due to the fact that Santayana has described the spiritual life in two opposite and incompatible ways: on the one hand, as a life of understanding, in which cognitive intent (itself a form of natural existence) is directed upon the ideals of truth and clarity of meaning; and on the other, as an escape from existence, as a disintoxication from all ideals, as a reversion to the immediately given that in itself possesses no meaning nor significance. From one point of view, the spiritual life is a life of knowing, marked by intent, engaged in inquiry, and one that achieves significant results in terms of that inquiry. For spirit "is not only the passive intuition implied in any essences being given, but also the understanding and belief that may greet their presence[SAF, p. 272]." The essences upon which the spiritual life will be directed will be meaningful objects, since they will be the outcome and the fulfilled enjoyment of preparatory processes of exploration and discovery, of definite procedures in physics or dialectic in discovering or constructing the forms which things embody or suggest. Its disinterestedness and detachment, moreover, will simply coincide with the spirit of impartiality and impersonality that animates all genuine scientific or theoretic inquiry.

From the second point of view, the spiritual life constitutes a mystical reversion to the immediate, in which the essences beheld in intuition are devoid of all meaning, precisely because they are cut off from the procedures or contexts in which they are brought into being or in terms of which they possess intelligible relations. The spiritual life will, then, not be distinguishable from an aesthetic idiocy nor a mystical absorption that finds salvation in contemplating pure blue or Pure Being. And the disintoxication that it boasts of will be nothing less than an acquiescence in the given state of moral or political affairs, an acquiescence that in effect expresses a despair of achieving rational ideals. If we emphasize the first of these approaches to the spiritual life, it will appear as but a refined extension of certain themes treated in *The Life of Reason*—the intrinsic values which the activities of the intellect in discovering the truth and of the imagination in conceiving ideal possibilities, possess for those who find their happiness in the exercise of these faculties. The contemplative life then becomes a form of ideal society, in Santayana's special use of that phrase in *Reason in Society,* the companionship of an individual with the themes of his imagination, the symbols devised by religion, art, and science for excellence, beauty, and truth. These themes or symbols become "precious not only for their representative or practical value, implying useful adjustments to the environing world, but even more, for their immediate or aesthetic power, for their kinship to the spirit they enlighten and exercise [LR, II, 197; cf. SE, pp. 119–22]." If we emphasize the second of the above approaches, the spiritual life becomes a form of postrational morality, falling into the same category with Christianity, Epicureanism, or Buddhism, and open to the same criticisms which Santayana himself has directed against these in *Reason in Science*. The one makes of the spiritual life the highest possible virtue of the mind, the other an obvious escape-mechanism. Let us consider these in turn.

The intellectual life.—Not only does the contemplative life itself constitute an ideal within a widely conceived life of reason, but its substance as well, in being composed of the natural interests of thought and imagination, will be directed upon the attainment of the specific ideals of these activities. For it will seek to understand the world in which we live, both in terms of its actual structure and in terms of the possible structures that the imagination can conceive. It will be a study of physics, or of those forms of natural existence which are actually embodied in the flux of events; and it will be a study of dialectic, or of those systems of logic, grammar, or poetic fancy which the imagination, taking its original suggestions from the actual materials of experience, will weave and construct in the form of possible rearrangements of those materials, ideally conceivable but not actually nor necessarily embodied in the flux of events. This theoretical investigation of the intelligible and imaginable forms of things will constitute an enterprise for which a certain detachment from the practical affairs of life is necessary in order that its results may be accomplished. Yet this detachment is only relative. It is a provisional disengagement from the types of seeking that animate men in their pursuit of material power, service, adventure, or love, in order that these, among other things, together with their underlying forces, their environment, and the ideals at which they aim may be all the more clearly understood. But the detachment cannot be universal and the disintoxication complete, since the understanding in whose interest this relative disengagement from practical affairs has been made, will possess its own ideals of truth, comprehensiveness, and depth of vision.

Therefore, although the realm of essences over which—as

Santayana sometimes claims—the spiritual life may range includes every possible form that sense, thought, fancy, or mystic insight may disclose—anarchic sense qualities like b flat,
toothache, or blue, the intelligible structures embodied in
existence and studied by the physical sciences, the abstract
languages and the imaginative vistas constructed by logic or
fancy, and the essence of Pure Being itself—it would seem
that if the spiritual life is to be genuinely intellectual, it must
confine itself to the middle range of these forms, to the realm
of the physically intelligible, the logically conceivable, and the
morally ideal. What lies outside these limits is either unen-
lightening or unimportant for a rational animal. "For while
the reward of action is contemplation or, in more modern
phrase, experience and consciousness, there is nothing stable
or interesting to contemplate except objects relevant to action
—the natural world and the mind's ideals[LR, V, 319]."

Neither the absorption in the immediacy of sensation nor
the mystical flight to the blank nothingness of Pure Being can
supplant the intellectual curiosity that seeks enlightenment
concerning the structures that control the movement of things
and the habits of men, the languages in terms of which that
movement or those habits may be described, and the moral
ends which may be served as a result of that enlightenment.
If the concern of the spiritual life is with essences, it is with
those which are the definable objects of discourse, the objects
of cognitive intent, those that possess logical implications and
that define the structure of some actual or possible fact. Even
its concern with possible facts is limited by the uses or relevance which a disclosure of those possibilities in knowledge
would have for practice and understanding. For

if dialectic takes a turn which makes it inapplicable in physics, which
makes it worthless for mastering experience, it loses all its dignity.
. . . The moral function and ultimate justification of dialectic is to
further the Life of Reason, in which human thought has the max-

imum practical validity, and may enjoy in consequence the richest ideal development [LR, V, 34].

Nothing would be gained by the privilege of surveying the entire realm of possibility in its absolute infinity (although a sense of this virtual infinity is sobering and enlightening to contemplation); as Aristotle put it, there are things which it is better not to know than to know.

As pure intuition is life at its best, when there is least rasping and thumping in its music, a prejudice or presumption arises that *any* essence is beautiful and life-enhancing. This platonic adoration of essence is undeserved. The realm of essence is dead, and the intuition of far the greater part of it would be deadly to any living creature [SAF, p. 130].

It is the contemplation of only so much of essence as is relevant or important to the endowed intellectual faculties of man that constitutes his genuine freedom of spirit (cf. PSL, pp. 41, 67–68; SAF, p. 276). The intuition of Pure Being consequently has no special status in the intellectual life, although in some quarters it is the most prized object of mystical contemplation and taken to be the goal of all spiritual insight. For when Pure Being is used as a synonym for the entire realm of imaginable forms in its infinity and absolute comprehensiveness, it becomes for a rational animal with limited faculties and interests, impossible and irrelevant to survey it in complete detail. When, on the other hand, Pure Being is simply a name for that universal quality which all conceivable forms possess, in so far as they are real "somewhat as light is in all colors or life in all feeling and thought," there again it possesses no preëminence as a subject for contemplation in the spiritual life.

In general, then, the spiritual life is not a release from preoccupation with existence, if by this anything more is meant than a provisional detachment from the pursuit of those activities which characterize the practical life. The spiritual life is itself an illustration of what natural existence flowers into when a form of consciousness has arisen that is capable of understanding with perfect clarity the conditions of its activity and the ideal possibilities of conduct.

That the fruition of happiness is intellectual . . . follows from the comprehensive scope of that intuition in which happiness is realized, a scope which distinguishes happiness from carnal pleasures; for . . . it is found in conceiving the total issue and ultimate fruits of life. . . . All experience can of course never be synthesized in act, because life is a passage and has many centres; yet such a synthesis is adumbrated everywhere; and when it is partially attained, in some reflective or far-seeing moment, it raises the mind to a contemplation which is very far from cold, being in fact ecstatic; yet this ecstasy remains intellectual in that it holds together the burden of many successive and disparate things, which in blind experience would exclude each other. . . . In raising truth to intuition of truth, in surveying the forms and places of many things at once and conceiving their movement, the intellect performs the most vital of possible acts, locks flying existence, as it were, in its arms and stands, all eyes and breathless, at the top of life [GTB, pp. 66–67].

Mysticism and post-rational morality.—The celebration of the contemplative life that Santayana's account presents, is disturbed, however, by the intrusion of certain doctrines which are open to serious criticism in terms of the very principles which Santayana himself at one time or another suggests. For certain of his characterizations of the spiritual life would make of it a form of mysticism and post-rational morality and thus exclude it from the structure of the life of reason.

Mysticism, as Santayana himself has analyzed it in *Poetry and Religion, The Sense of Beauty,* and *The Life of Reason,* arises when, perceiving the conventionality and relativity of all human ideas and values, an attempt is made to overthrow such categories of thought and action. Mysticism functions as a principle of dissolution. And the grounds of this destructive movement may be considered under two heads, epistemological and moral. On the first count, the mystic is impressed by the fact that all our ideas and interpretations of nature are obtained through the faculties of sense, understanding, and imagination, which, being human, are therefore taken to be infected with relativity, conventionality, and subjectivity. These faculties he insists, inevitably color their material with a bias and an illusory perspective that form no part of its original essence. The mystic's interest, therefore, becomes one of identifying himself with a surrounding "total reality," the disclosure of which is unaffected by the finitude and partiality of human perspective.

The way of true wisdom, therefore, if true wisdom is to deal with the Absolute, can only lie in abstention; neither the senses nor the common understanding, and much less the superstructure raised upon these by imagination, logic, or tradition, must delude us: we must keep our thoughts fixed upon the inanity of all this in comparison with the unthinkable truth, with the undivided and unimaginable reality. Everything, says the mystic, is nothing, in comparison with the One[PR, p. 14].

On the side of moral values, the same principle of dissolution, directed to the specific and biased nature of all experience of value, is an attempt to escape moral discriminations and preference. Values, the mystic (rightly enough) insists, are relative to the limited natural impulses lying at their base; yet his consuming passion, rather, is with a supreme and absolute value that shall not be infected with human bias. The mystic's cure for the illusions and partialities of human striving lies in rescinding all such human and passionate interests.

Any special interest, any claim made by a finite and mortal creature upon an infinite world, is bound to be defeated. It is not special acts . . . which are sinful, but action and will themselves that are intrinsically foolish[LR, III, 205].

Just as on an intellectual plane this type of mysticism involves a denial of validity to all representative ideas, so on a moral plane it advocates a revulsion from all selected ideals.

Now the interesting and curious fact is that if we substitute much of Santayana's account in the later works of the Realm of Essence as it figures for the spiritual life for the "absolute" of the above quotation, and his doctrines of a complete "disintoxication of values" and the "absolute Good" of spiritual insight for the mystic's program of moral abstention, we find that the situation is not at all changed. Santayana's later analysis of the spiritual life fits exactly, almost point for point, the mysticism he was himself at one time so eager to condemn.

In the volume, *Scepticism and Animal Faith,* Santayana describes the approach to essence through skepticism with respect to beliefs and assertions about objects in the external environment. Knowledge of such objects is a claim to reveal their properties; it is "a form of belief in things absent or eventual." Such knowledge is necessary to man as an animal in constant interaction with an outer world. He needs to be informed about the course that events will or might take, in order to prepare to meet or to modify them. But such information as knowledge yields is always open to doubt; it is constantly exposed to all sorts of errors, arising both from attributing to things properties not intrinsically possessed by them, and from viewing such objects in perspectives that are inevitably colored by the shifting or changing organs of the observer. The skeptic, in realizing these facts, will reduce the presumptive claim of knowledge to reveal the truth about the environment, the past, and the future, to the mere terms of these beliefs, to the essences involved in such descriptions. Ultimately nothing but these essences will remain, after all reference to the existence of outlying objects or to a conscious organism making these claims has been denied all validity. They will constitute the sole realities of intuition and be nothing but immediate presences, luminously obvious, immaterial, and insignificant of anything beyond. Knowledge, which for a rational animal is a symbolic description of and faith in the disclosure of the truth about material objects, will be reduced to a pure intuition of essences.

Now we need not stop here to point out the inadequacies of this argument, to show, for example, that the fact of the relativity of knowledge to human organs is no warrant for distrusting their information; nor to show that the essence of the only valid skepticism is the methodological skepticism of science, that challenges the evidence for any single proposition only in order to supplant it with more adequate evidence gathered by the same standard techniques that are throughout employed in inquiry, and not a wholesale skepticism that would overthrow science altogether; nor to show, finally, that the symbolic character of knowledge, which is eventually reinstated on the grounds of animal faith, is not the sort described, but is realistic rather than Lockian. All these facts have either been touched upon already or constitute the subject matter for a special inquiry. What is significant for our present purpose is the fact that the transcendental and skeptical approach which Santayana adopts and which, for the spiritual life, affords one avenue to the intuition of the realm of essence, is precisely similar to the mystical claim to have reached a form of reality that is at once superior to the knowledge obtained in ordinary investigation and free from the taint of human subjectivity and relativity. For, he tells us,

to consider an essence is, from a spiritual point of view, to enlarge acquaintance with true being; but it is not even to broach knowledge of fact; and the ideal object so defined may have no natural significance, though it has aesthetic immediacy and logical definition. The modest scope of this speculative acquaintance with essence renders it infallible, whilst the logical and aesthetic ideality of its object renders that object eternal [SAF, p. 75].

We may note, to begin with, that while Santayana is correct in claiming aesthetic immediacy for essences beheld in intuition, it is questionable whether the property of logical definition can be attributed to them, since such definition is a function of cognitive or dialectical intent, something which, on his own premises, is definitely related to the acts of a psyche rather than that of a "free" spirit. When carried to the limit, therefore, a retreat to the immediately given (which is taken to be one of the marks of the spiritual life) is in reality an abstention from all thought and a wiping out of all recognized distinctions in the intelligible structure of nature. It means a return to the innocence of rudimentary consciousness, rather than an advance along the road of discriminating intelligence. Since the objects of intuition will be wholly immediate, they will be devoid of all logical implication, transitive reference, or cognitive value. Instead of being the forms of definable discourse or the objects of significant imagination, they will be the marks of arrested intelligence, brute sensation, or meaningless dreams. Articulation and rational vision consequently will be impossible. The immediate is at the opposite pole from intelligibility.

Nor will the supposed ultimate reality of essences be thereby disclosed. The ultimacy of essences is not that of an antecedent realm of being, prior to all cognitive or material realization, but the concomitant existence of form inherent in nature, thought, or imagination. To recognize these forms through intelligence, consequently, it is neither necessary nor consistent to disparage ordinary knowledge in favor of intuition. It is not necessary, since those forms cannot be attained through any other means; and it is inconsistent, since "in throwing over all human ideas, because they are infected with humanity, all human ideas are being sacrificed to one of them —the idea of an absolute reality [PR, p. 12]." The conception of the realm of essence, the dream of Platonism, is no less and no more the product of human thinking than any other. Thus the immediacy of essences prevents the spiritual life from being genuinely cognitive, whereas the supposed ontologic ultimacy and priority of essences are simply the result of giving selective emphasis to a single phase of human experience in relative disregard and disparagement of its other phases.

If as a theory of intellectual ideals Santayana's description of the spiritual life is inadequate, it is no less so when considered in relation to the sphere of moral interests. The spiritual life, Santayana tells us, differs from the life of the natural or worldly man, in escaping the urgency and passion of animal interests and values; it marks a disintoxication from their influence (PSL, p. 30). For a value is something relative to a particular interest, expressing the importance which things acquire in virtue of the benefit or satisfaction which they bring to an animal having a particular material basis or bias. To this urgency and precariousness of moral behavior, spirit is essentially foreign, since it has no special moral interest in proclaiming one interest in preference to some other. It is the mark of spirit to be disillusioned of all moral ideals, to treat every good pursued anywhere and by anybody as the manifestation of some essence that has the same ontologic status as any other in the realm of essence.

The intellect from the beginning is "speculative and impartial in its own outlook, and thinks it not robbery to take the point of view of God, of the truth, and of eternity [GTB, p. 65]." The proper function of spirit, in passing beyond good and evil, is "to see such things as come in its way under the form of eternity, in their intrinsic character and relative value, in a word, in their truth [PSL, pp. 33; cf. *ibid., pp.* 42, 53]." Of all things, therefore, spirit is not practical; it is impartial in its vision. It has no interest in bringing things about, no interest, that is, in reforming the actual. The form that the actual already bears is sufficient for its contemplative enjoyment. "Spirit is merciful and tender because it has no private motive to make it spiteful; yet it is unflinchingly austere because it cannot make any private motive its own [PSL, p. 31]." While practical reason is admittedly biased and relative to various particular interests whose spokesman it is, and among which it attempts to establish some harmony, spirit, on the other hand, is completely standpointless with respect to such interests.

Pure spirit [says Santayana] "would be lame, and evidently biassed by some biological accident, if it did not love every good loved anywhere by anybody. . . . Every good pursued is genuinely good, and the perfection of every creature equally perfection. Every good therefore is a good forever to a really clarified, just, and disinterested spirit [OS, pp. 291–92].

The natural life is morally rooted and biased, the spiritual life is disinterested and free. The proper object of its devotion is a universal good, the "sum" of all possible perfections, infinitely various, to which all living things aspire. For the spirit, such a universal good is a symbol of that invariant element of goodness which pervades all particular goods. "Universal good is something dispersed, various, contrary to itself in its opposite embodiments; nevertheless, to the mystic, it seems a single living object, the One Beloved, a good to be embraced all at once, finally and forever, leaving not the least shred of anything outside [OS, p. 293]."

The first point, with respect to this account of the spiritual life, upon which we may fix our attention as demanding some clarification is that which has reference to what Santayana evidently takes as a distinguishing mark of that life, namely its "disintoxication from values." For it would seem that if we are to take this as a serious claim to having overcome completely the necessity for distinguishing good from evil, on all levels of vital endeavor, then we are left with an evident contradiction. For if we grant, as Santayana asks us to do, that the proper function of spirit "is to see such things as come in its way under the form of eternity, in their transitiveness and necessity, in a word, in their truth[PSL, p. 33]," then evidently the good of the intellect, which consists precisely in this ability to see things in their necessity and their truth, remains as one value from which there can be no disintoxication, as one ideal that demands efforts for its realization. And the good of the intellect is no more and no less a good than that which satisfies any other natural interest of life.

It is impossible, in short, to be mystical "all around." This needs to be emphasized, for despite all talk about disintoxication from values, it still remains true that the disintoxication itself is but with respect to certain values, while leaving others intact. It is impossible to negate all ideals and to elude all interests except by death. And as Santayana himself remarks, in connection with the mystical efforts of post-rational moralities:

As a matter of fact, animal instincts and natural standards of excellence are never eluded in them, for no moral experience has other terms; but the part of the natural ideal which remains active appears in opposition to all the rest and, by an intelligible illusion, seems to be no part of that natural ideal because, compared with the commoner passions on which it reacts, it represents some simpler or more attenuated hope—the appeal to some very humble or very much chastened satisfaction, or to an utter change in the conditions of life. . . . The renunciation of the will must stop at the point where the will to be saved makes its appearance: and as this desire may be no less troublesome and insistent than any other, as it may even become a tormenting obsession, the mystic is far from the end of his illusions when he sets about to dispel them. There is one rational method to which, in post-rational systems, the world is still thought to be docile, one rational endeavour which nature is sure to crown with success. This is the method of deliverance from existence, the effort after salvation. . . . The pretension to have reached a point of view from which *all* impulse may be criticized is accordingly an untenable pretension [LR, V, 266, 287, 289].

All this is rather obvious and, as we may see, something which Santayana himself admits, even in his own descriptions of the spiritual life as a life of knowing. He tends to ignore these facts, however, when, after having instituted a sharp distinction between the will and the intellect, after the manner of Schopenhauer (cf. SB, p. 37) or Christian ethics, he removes all desire and intent from the latter. But, according to a naturalistic psychology, such dualism is unwarranted, since desire or will operates on all levels of thought and conduct and constitutes the basis for discriminating the specific goods and evils that would satisfy or thwart those interests.

There are, however, other aspects to Santayana's description of the spiritual life which reveal an even closer kinship to systems of post-rational morality and which remove all doubt, therefore, that we are dealing with an ideal incompatible with the principles of rational ethics. We may see this clearly if we compare the account of the spiritual life given by Santayana in his later writings with that of spirituality given by him in *Reason in Religion*. For as described in the latter, spirituality marks a devotion to selected ideal ends, guided by and based on piety or a recognition of and loyalty to the necessary material forces of life and nature. To be spiritual in this view is not to renounce life's interests. On the contrary, it is to accept them in all their fullness and urgency, simply refining and imaginatively elaborating their genuine purposes in order to make of them a rational whole. The spiritual man is one who has become conscious of his ideals and is devoted to the perfection of the materials of his life. A man is "spiritual when he envisages his goal so frankly that his whole material life becomes a transparent and transitive vehicle, an instrument which scarcely arrests attention but allows the spirit to use it economically and with perfect detachment and freedom [LR, III, 193–94]." A spiritual man can be said to be not-worldly only in the sense in which this term signifies the avoidance of a blind subservience to the instrumentalities of life. The aim of spirituality is the same as that of intelligence in its analysis and clarification of ideals. To lead the spiritual life is to understand and to act in accordance with that which is morally relevant to life as a whole. Ideals acquire validity in their applicability to material conduct and affairs. The spiritual man is not apart from the world; rather by his elevated and penetrating vision he is brought into closer contact with its essential and ultimate values.

Santayana's later account of the spiritual life is markedly different from this earlier description, in that it tends to substitute a stoic conformity to and acquiescence in the given state of moral or political affairs, for the genuinely intelligent piety of the rational life; and even where it would rise above a pantheistic identification of the good with the actual, it seeks refuge not in some selected and finite conception of the good that would serve as a concrete ideal for practice, but rather in a mystical and wholly abstract intuition of the Good.

The naturalistic recognition of the relativity of all ideals to their finite and irrational conditions tends to become for the disinterested attitude of the spiritual life an occasion for tolerance and irony, and in the end a willingness to conform to whatever social conditions happen to prevail, since some allegiance, even when it is a matter of mere habit or custom, is necessary for one who would be a member of a given social group. The irony that arises from the awareness of the fact that but for some change in the accidental station assumed in the world, one might have had entirely different allegiances, and the tolerance that results from the admission that all ideals are in their natural origin equally necessary, results in a point of view which comes dangerously close to pantheism. For in attempting to overcome the necessity imposed on every living creature for distinguishing good from evil (these terms signifying the functions which things bear relatively to the interests which they either support or hinder), a view results which regards all ideals as equally ideal, since all are necessary and justifiable naturally (cf. EGP, p. 123).

Yet this all-inclusive charity toward every possible good, besides tending to obliterate the distinction between physics and morals, tends in the end to serve as a justification for whatever pre-rational, barbarous ideals may happen to exist. And when we find Santayana telling us that "understanding relieves a truly intelligent man from fussiness about social institutions and conventions [because] they are absurd [GTB, p. 71]," we seem to be confronted with an apologetic for reigning conventions and a willingness to submit to the powers that be, that cannot but appear as the very abdication of intelligence in the face of irrationality. It leaves the field open for all sorts of fanaticisms to arise and contest for domination in the world. Spirituality may thus come to justify or condone indirectly, yet tragically, those forces in society that are intent upon the destruction of all that liberal civilization holds dear, and ultimately therefore, the very conditions for the exercise of genuinely intellectual interests themselves.

Nor can the conception of a universal good, the sum and essence of all possible goods beheld in mystical insight, come to relieve the suspicion we may have that the spiritual life has become pantheistic. For even if Santayana tells us that in saluting every good pursued everywhere, the religion of a clarified spirit does not involve the belief that all such goods are in fact actualized in the world, but rather that "to love things spiritually . . . means to love the love in them, to worship the good which they pursue, and to see them all prophetically in their possible beauty [OS, p. 292]"—we are driven to ask what the possible content of such an idea can be, and what value it can possess for a rational animal confronted with the necessity of choosing definite and selected goods every moment of life. The concept of a universal good, like the concept of Pure Being, represents the last stage of an abstraction that removes all significant content from the objects of our contemplation or interest. It cannot suffice for guiding the possible ideal of rational living, since in being entirely empty, precisely because it is infinitely charitable, it removes an essential condition for all rational ideals, their being sacrificial and restrictive. Whereas piety for the rational life is an acknowledgment of the specific sources of our activity and a use of particular instruments for the achievement of ends, and spirituality a devotion to selected, finite ideals, piety for the spiritual life becomes rather a submissive humility in the face of a total, universal power (the realm of matter), and spirituality a mystic contemplation of a universal good that has no relevant content nor directions for the specific interests of a given life.

In general, post-rational systems of morality are distinguished by the fact that they express a despair of attaining a rational morality. Historically they find expression during a period of decline and social or political disintegration, after the experiment in rational living "has been tried and found wanting," as was the case, for example, with the Stoics and the Epicureans following the debacle of Athens and the Periclean Age. "In a decadent age, the philosopher who surveys the world and sees that the end of it is even as the beginning, may not feel that the intervening episode, in which he and all he values after all figure, is worth consideration and he may cry, in his contemplative spleen, that *all* is vanity [LR, V, 264]." Santayana's portrayal of the spiritual life reflects a similar despair in the face of the confusion and barbarism of the present world.

The occasion for Santayana's earlier attraction to the post-rational aspects of the spiritual life, as expressed in *Lucifer* and some of the minor works of that period, is to be found in the attempt to find consolation in beauty, in the face of an alien mechanical world pictured by nineteenth-century physical and biologic science. Religion had been dislodged from its authoritative and dominating rôle in men's lives. What better thing to do than to accept the stark and bitter "truth," adopt an attitude of stoic conformity to the inevitable and ultimately irrational laws of nature, and to find refuge in an Epicurean delight in the figments of sense and fancy? In the *Life of Reason*, we find Santayana attempting a reinterpretation of spiritual values in the light of a fundamental naturalism, adapting the moral idealism of traditional schemes of values to given needs of man's biological and social nature. Its outlook of hopefulness for artistic and social creativity, allied with its consciousness of the worth of knowledge as power, reflect the upward beat and expanding economy of a culture possessed of increased productive and technologic means. But whereas in the earlier writings the stimulus for adopting a contemplative attitude was the confrontation of the world-view of science with that of religion, in the latest writings, it is the increased confusion of the social world, reflecting a maladjustment of political and economic forces, that gives ground for the attempt to rise to an otherworldly contemplation of essences and a complete disintoxication from moral values. Confronted with an increase in irrationality, physical force, conflict, and dissolution, the mind turns to some theory of virtue that will lift it above and allow it to transcend such facts. Readjustment is no longer sought in a renewed effort to envisage the ideal forms of action and social behavior, but by laying up one's treasures in another world.

The charity this new attitude offers is, in effect, an admission of the defeat awaiting any rational ideal. "Charity is less than philanthropy in that it expects the defeat of man's natural desires and accepts that defeat; and it is more than philanthropy in that, in the face of defeat, it brings consolation [DL, p. 139]." In common with Christianity, such an attitude tends to set up a dualism between the body and the mind, the flesh and the spirit, and to place the instruments for salvation in the latter rather than in the former. Like the otherworldly emphasis of Christianity, Santayana's conception of the spiritual life recalls the spirit from its concern with the intelligible structure of nature and the natural ideals of human life, to a world beyond. It is essentially a variant of the advice to render unto Caesar those things that are Caesar's and to God the things that are God's, and of the belief that the Kingdom of God is within us.

The realm of essence to which the spirit is recalled is a world of Platonic Ideas that has been romantically extended in infinite directions. Happiness is now sought in the free play of fancy that can roam undisturbed and joyful among strangely novel, distant, and different worlds, the varied imaginative excursions into which are to be enjoyed in their immediacy as subjective impressions, significant as indications neither of natural conditions nor of possible moral ideals. Whereas in the life of reason the imagination is subjected to a rational discipline that adjusts its dreams to relevant facts and moral ideals, in the spiritual life the imagination is subjected to no such demands. Occam's razor is denounced as an unnecessary and pauperizing instrument for shearing the mind of its fuzzy growths. And just as Epicureanism, in Santayana's words, cut itself off from "politics, religion, enterprise and passion" and therefore came to express the "genuine sentiment of persons, at once mild and emancipated who find themselves floating on the ebb-tide of some civilization, and enjoying its fruits, without any longer representing the forces that brought that civilization about [LR, V, 270–71]," so too the ethics of the spiritual life may be looked upon as occupying a similar status.

Summary and conclusion.—If one surveys Santayana's

philosophy as a whole, I think it may be said that its essential interest has been to unite a thoroughgoing appreciation of the material aspects of being and conduct with an equally thoroughgoing emphasis upon the ideal and imaginative phases of experience. These terms, however, receive definite content and significance only when we note the specific manner in which they are employed in the various parts of his philosophy or the stages of its development. For the manner in which they are combined is not the same throughout, but instead reveals the different aspects and selective emphases of his thought.

In the genuinely naturalistic portions of his system, nature provides the ultimate setting for rational action and theoretic inquiry. Nature is an order of substances and events, of beginnings and endings, of powers and their fulfillments. The essences of things are those that can be disclosed in cognitive experience as describing their constitutions and relations. All structures and ideals have a natural ground. Metaphysically the relation of essence and existence is that of form inhering in some subject matter, where this subject matter constitutes either the realm of physical objects or the objects of creative thought and imagination. In either case essences come into being with the productive energies of nature and cannot have being prior to or independently of these energies. Morally the ideal is an outgrowth of the actual, exhibiting the fulfillment of a clarified will. The objects of intellectual contemplation are the principles of natural processes and the ideals of human conduct, both of which are found latently contained in some already existing subject matter, needing but the refined techniques of science and philosophy to make them the explicit objects of intelligent regard. Methodologically the results of inquiry are the outcome of procedures in which the raw material of common sense and ordinary perception serve as the sources from which the principles that describe the forms of things take their start and to which they return for their applicability. The rational or ideal in all cases is thus an emanation or concomitant aspect of natural forces.

In the dualistic portions of Santayana's system these relations between existence and essence, the actual and the ideal, idea and fact, are either reversed or rendered equivocal. Essences become hypostatized into a world set apart, subsisting eternally prior to the realm of matter and possessing an inviolate status, apart from all connection with the actual course of natural events. Morally the realm of matter encompasses action that needs to be made rational only as a concession to the necessity for living at all. The ultimate ideal, however, is not an outgrowth of the natural desires of man, but an escape from those desires to the infinite and immediate forms antecedently and eternally subsisting in their own realm. And methodologically knowledge, when it does arise, is not a revelation of the structure of things, but a form of conventional madness that needs to be cultivated only as a concession to action, but which in the absence of such necessity would better have been reduced to an immediate intuition of essences.

Santayana, in reviewing the point of view indigenous to Christianity, remarks that according to that view

all history was henceforth essentially nothing but the conflict between these two cities [the City of God and the City of Satan]; two moralities, one natural, the other supernatural; two philosophies, one rational, the other revealed; two beauties, one corporeal, the other spiritual; two glories, one temporal, the other eternal; two institutions, one the world, the other the Church. These, whatever their momentary alliances or compromises, were radically opposed and fundamentally alien to one another [LR, III, 95–96].

Something of the same estimate must be made of Santayana's own philosophy. It exhibits in the course of its development an alternation between attitudes that, however much they may seem to borrow one from the other, are basically and inevitably opposed. For it exhibits two points of view that allow each one to criticize the other: the one being worldly, naturalistic, humanistic, Aristotelian; the other otherworldly, supernatural, dualistic, Platonic. Yet no ultimate synthesis or mixture such as Santayana evidently seeks is possible. For the one point of view, the will expressing itself in a spontaneous and varied experience is chastened rationally in the light of its material conditions and ideal goals. For the other, the spirit disciplined in its denial of material wants, sees all things given in a varied and imaginative experience as illustrations of infinite Being. The one is a morality of humanism and intelligent practice, the essence of Greek ethics; the other is an ethics of quietism and resignation, insight animated by a spirit of disillusionment and irony, the essence of oriental mysticism. The moral sensitiveness to and sincere adoption of such divergent views is testimony to the range and acuteness of Santayana's mind. Yet it is as a naturalist and Aristotelian that, we venture to think, Santayana's thought will win for him the respect and admiration which its penetrating vision, sanity, and comprehensiveness deserve. As for the rest, it still may be appreciated as a work of imagination expressing the sentiments and fancies of a mind too engrossed in the beauties of a dialectic and the persuasiveness of a moral attitude to perceive that neither the dialectic nor the attitude can be taken as a valid picture of the world or of man's genuinely ideal place in it.

INDEX